Felt Wonderland

Felt Wonderland

FELTMAKING TECHNIQUES AND 12 FANTASY-INSPIRED PROJECTS

Lisa Marie Olson

SEARCH PRESS

First published in 2018

Search Press Limited
Wellwood, North Farm Road,
Tunbridge Wells, Kent TN2 3DR

Photographs by Stacy Grant

Additional photographs by Paul Bricknell:
6 (top two), 10, 11, 12, 13, 16, 17, 18–28, 30–33, 35, 36,
38, 39 (excl. bl), 40, 41, 46, 48, 49 (excl. br), 52, 53 (excl.
br), 55, 56 (excl. bl), 57 (excl. br), 61, 62, 64, 66 (excl. bl), 67
(excl. tr), 68, 70 (excl. bl+r), 71 (excl. br), 72 (excl. tr), 73, 76,
77 (excl. br), 78, 80, 81 (excl. tr), 84, 86, 88, 90 (excl. br),
91, 94 (excl. b), 95 (excl. bl), 96.

Text copyright © Lisa Marie Olson 2018
Design copyright © Search Press Ltd 2018

ISBN: 978-1-78221-511-0

Suppliers
For details of suppliers, please visit the
Search Press website: www.searchpress.com

Publisher's note
All the step-by-step photographs in this book
feature the author, Lisa Marie Olson. No models
have been used.

For further inspiration and information, please visit:
Website: tigerlilymakes.co.uk
Facebook: Tigerlily Makes

Printed in China through Asia Pacific Offset

Acknowledgements

My thanks are due to:

My editor, May Corfield, for providing the most
supportive and helpful environment to flourish in
and Search Press for giving me the opportunity to
do what I love doing the most;

Craig De Souza at AFCI for supporting my work
and providing a great platform to connect with
industry specialists;

World of Wool for providing great customer service,
speedy delivery and the most deliciously coloured
array of wool!

Angela Burman of Burman Bears for nurturing my
creative talent and giving me the confidence to
take the next big step forward.

Contents

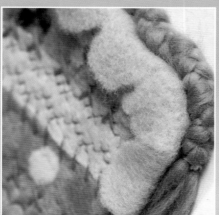

Introduction

My love affair with creative arts started at school with needlework and textile art. I quickly realised that I had a natural flair and ability to create wonderful things with threads, fabric, ribbons, buttons and leftover bits and bobs, and my interest grew from there.

Felt Wonderland is a complete guide to wet felting, from basic feltmaking techniques that show you how to make a piece of flat felt, to the more advanced techniques which allow a more three-dimensional result.

Many of my designs are created and inspired by a great love of classic stories and fairy tales, such as *Alice's Adventures in Wonderland* and *The Chronicles of Narnia*. They were very much my escape as a child. *Felt Wonderland* is inspired by Lewis Carroll's classic story *Alice's Adventures in Wonderland*, which shows us a world where everything is not quite what it seems. In the story, Alice grows and shrinks in size when she takes a drink from the 'Drink Me' bottle – and the world around her changes accordingly. This is reflected in the oversized roses on the teacups on pages 88–91, for example, and the undersized rose on the teapot on pages 92–95.

It was Alice and the other characters that jumped off the page and sparked my ever-busy imaginative mind. Most of the project titles are connected to the characters in the original novel, such as Tilly's Teacups (Tilly being one of the dormice) and the Queen of Hearts Egg Cosy. I hope you enjoy making the felt and the Alice-inspired projects in this book.

Lisa Marie x

Tools & materials

Merino wool

Merino wool is a fine, super soft wool that comes from a breed of sheep that originated in Spain, although the modern merino breed was domesticated in New Zealand, Australia and parts of Africa. The term merino is widely used in the textile industry, and it tends to be dyed for commercial use. Also known as roving, tops or fleece, it is commonly used in felt making, spinning and knitting.

Due to its ultra-fine fibres, merino wool is great for blending with other fibres, such as silk. Merino in an array of beautiful colours is used for all the projects within this book. Merino fibres are soft and malleable and therefore this type of wool allows for a wide range of wet felted projects, some of which are completely seamless and require no stitching at all.

It is important to bear in mind that not all merino wool is produced ethically, and so research into ethical producers has been a big influence on my decision about where to source my wool. I only source from well-known and trusted suppliers who have a good environmental policy in place to limit and reduce the impact of the production of merino.

Colours

For the projects in this book, I have used the colour names that refer to the brand of merino (from World of Wool, an online store) that I have used in the book. If you are using a different brand, please refer to the project photographs for guidance on colours, or use colours of your choice.

Pre-felt

Pre-felt is wool that has been partially felted, usually on an industrial scale, by needle punching dry fibres. It has a versatile range of uses for wet felting, needle felting, 3D felting and a whole host of other crafts.

It is generally bought in coloured sheets that you can cut up or shape according to your requirements. In this book it has been used to create flower embellishments on the Alice Peg Bag (see page 64), for wet felting decorative detail on the Maisy Daisy Handbag (see page 60) and for needle embellishing decorative detail on the Tigerlily Lampshade (see page 68).

You can also buy handmade pre-felt, which is made with two or more layers of wool roving, tops or fleece. This is then wet felted, using soap and warm water, enough for the fibres to catch together but not to fuse completely into solid felt. Handmade pre-felt usually comes in slightly more interesting shades than needle-punched pre-felt.

Embroidery threads

I have used an array of pretty embroidery threads to add decorative stitched detail to a number of projects throughout this book, such as the Snowdrop Cottage Sewing Case (see page 46), the Maisy Daisy Handbag (see page 60) and the Wonderland Teapot (see page 92).

I chose to use embroidery threads produced by DMC because they come in an amazing range of colours and are super soft and shiny, although there are many other brands available that are equally good. I use stranded cotton, which is a fine, long staple cotton comprising six easily divisible strands. Using different numbers of strands allows you to vary the weight of your stitches. In this book I have chosen to use all six strands together, to add visible depth and detail to the hand-felted projects.

Other equipment

Bamboo mat

A bamboo mat is used for agitating and shrinking the wool fibres, which is an important part of the process. A mat that is approximately 95cm long and 45cm wide (37½ x 17¾in) will be fine for the lampshade, which is the largest project. You may wish to have a smaller mat as well, which you may find easier to use for smaller projects.

Washing-up liquid

Just a dash of this is needed in the water bottle to encourage the fibres to attach to each other. As a general guide, one or two squirts of liquid into a 450ml bottle full of warm water should be fine. You can use this in addition to a bar of soap.

Washing-up liquid bottle

An old, clean bottle is invaluable for holding soapy water when felting. Squirt it onto the wool as you go.

Soap

Soap mixed with water is used to help the fibres attach to each other and helps to speed up the felting process. Any bar/brand of soap will work; I tend to use handmade soap, as it's kinder on the skin.

Nylon curtain netting

This is an essential piece of equipment. Nylon curtain netting is used to cover the wool before the agitation process begins. Anything else will cause problems with the felt attaching itself to the covering rather than to itself. It is much easier to detangle wool from a synthetic material such as nylon than it is from other coverings.

Dishcloth

I use a dishcloth to help push the soapy water through the fibres.

Towel

An old towel is useful to place under the bamboo mat to save your work surface from getting soaked.

Felting needles

These are long, barbed industrial-type needles. The barbs, or grooves, go along the needle shaft and face downwards. This helps to push the fibres into the surface and prevents them from pulling back out of the project you are working on.

Needle felting pad

This provides an effective surface to work against when creating needle embellishment. It helps to protect the needle and limits needle breakage with its soft, spongy surface. It is usually made of high-density foam.

Hot glue gun

Glue guns are particularly useful for attaching embellishments to felt as stitching can sometimes work its way loose. Felt is a non-woven cloth and doesn't have a weave as such for the stitches to hold on to.

Ballpoint pen and erasable marker pen

A ballpoint pen is used for drawing around templates. Projects that have visible non-stitched edges need to be marked using an erasable marker pen.

Ruler

This is useful for measuring and keeping an eye on shrinkage/sizing.

Scissors

These are essential to cut pre-felt or to cut out stitched projects and embellishments such as flowers, as well as embroidery or sewing thread.

Pinking shears

These allow you to create pretty edges to embellishments.

Sewing needle

This is used to sew felt pieces together and to sew any decorative surface embroidery onto projects.

Metal dies

Dies are metal shapes that can be used with manual die-cutting machines to help you create perfect edges or more accuracy in your projects. These are optional.

Coat hanger

A coat hanger is used in the Alice Peg Bag project (see page 64).

Double-sided sticky foam mount pads

These are required to raise certain areas of projects to create a more 3D look.

Thick chenille sticks/floristry wire

I used these to create the decorative edging around the Wonderland Teapot lid (see page 95).

Shadow frame

This is a deep box picture frame that can be used to display your project.

Plastic resist sheeting

Any smooth, thick plastic, such as PVC pond liner (available from DIY stores) is ideal for making templates. Essential for making seamless projects, it will prevent one side of the project from felting to the other.

Vinyl flooring offcuts

Thicker than plastic resist sheeting, this material makes templates for more 3D seamless projects, such as bowls or teapots.

Slipper lasts

A 'last' is a solid shape around which a shoe or slipper is moulded. It provides you with a surface on which to create slippers. Lasts are usually moulded from polystyrene.

Sew-on slipper soles

These are optional, but advisable from a safety point of view when wearing slippers. They also make the slippers more hard-wearing.

Plastic food bags

These are used to cover the slipper lasts so that the felt doesn't adhere to the polystyrene.

Water-soluble fabric

This is ideal for creating motifs on felt, as it is virtually impossible to embroider directly onto felt. Simply pin the fabric to the felt, embroider your motif directly onto it, then wash away the fabric.

Toy stuffing

This is made from hygienic polyester and is perfect for projects that need a bit of stuffing.

Lampshade kit

A kit is useful when making felt lampshades as it comes with everything you need and gives you a size to work to.

Double-sided sticky tape

I used this to attach the felt to the lampshade ring in the Tigerlily Lampshade project (see page 68).

Embroidery hoop

I used this to embroider the rose motif for the Alice Peg Bag project (see page 64). It also helped me to centre the motif accurately.

Hook and loop dots

Also known as touch fasteners, I used these handy fastenings for the Snowdrop Cottage Sewing Case (see page 46).

Hand cream

If you do a lot of wet felting, this will help to soothe your hands afterwards.

Embellishments and finishing details

Embellishments come in all shapes, sizes and styles, and I have used a wide array of items from ribbons to buttons and sparkly pearls, in colours to complement the colour palette of the projects.

Embellishments can also be things you have made yourself; for example, the little flower embellishments on the Alice Peg Bag (see page 64) or the rose on the Wonderland Teapot (see page 92). Embellishments give you the freedom to personalise and customise your projects. Half the fun of embellishing projects comes from choosing, matching and styling the embellishments.

Ribbon

Ribbon comes in all widths, colours and patterns so is very versatile. It's a great way to add a little accent to your project. I have used it on the teapot and one of the egg cosies (see left and right).

Flat-back pearls and silver rim pearls

These make excellent flower centres and come in a wide range of colours and sizes (see left and right).

Mini playing cards

These were a perfect addition to the Mad as a Hatter Egg Cosy (see right) and are easily available online.

Satin piping

Satin piping gives a touch of luxury to an item and the smooth, shiny surface contrasts well with the matt felt (see below).

Buttons

Buttons are an invaluable embellishment and I have used them on the Footman Baby Boy Slippers (see page 82) and Mary Anna's Pincushion (see page 50).

Pompom trim

This is a fantastic edging and I have used it on my pincushion stack (see page 50) to contrast it with the other cushions.

Decorative wooden dolly pegs

Continuing the slightly retro theme of the Alice Peg Bag (see page 64), with its vintage-style apron, I have used old-fashioned dolly pegs with it (see below). These are easily available and can be painted to match your project.

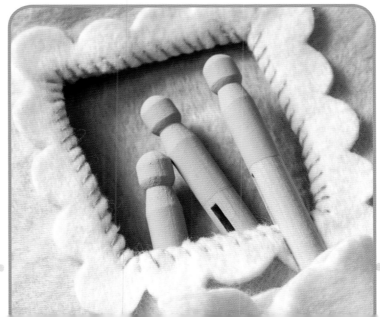

Techniques

Wet felting

Wet felting is a process by which cloth is formed when soap and water are added to raw wool fleece and the fibres are agitated. Agitation causes the fibre to mat and compress together to form cloth. Felt is an unwoven cloth and as far as it is known, it is the only form of unwoven cloth in existence. Flat felt can be used for embellishments such as flowers and leaves, as well as for whole items.

   Here we are going to go through the process of making a piece of flat felt.

How to get started

You will need a towel, a bamboo mat, a piece of nylon netting, washing-up liquid, an empty washing-up liquid bottle, soap, a dishcloth, merino wool and you are ready to go.

   To make a piece of flat felt it is important to start off with the basics and make sure you master the technique of pulling even wisps of fleece.

Making a piece of flat felt

1 Hold the fleece in your left hand approximately 7.5cm (3in) down from the top of the fleece as in the picture; place your right hand over the top of the wispy bits, being careful not to scrunch them up. Make sure that the fingers on your right hand are pointing straight down.

2 Holding firmly with your left hand at the lower part of the fleece pull with your right hand to release a fine, even wisp of fleece. NB: if you are left-handed simply follow this technique with your right hand at the bottom and your left hand at the top.

Laying the fleece horizontally

1 Begin to lay the fleece on the bamboo mat wisp by wisp in a horizontal direction, as shown. As you pull more wisps off, you will have to nudge your hand down the fleece bit by bit, to sustain the evenness.

2 Cover the majority of the bamboo mat and press your hands over the fleece to check that there are no areas that are too fine or have holes in them.

Laying the fleece vertically

3 Just as you did for the horizontal layer, pull fine even wisps of fleece and lay them down vertically to create a second layer.

4 Continue laying the fleece vertically until you have covered the entire first layer with fleece. Next, cover the fleece with nylon netting and you are ready to start wetting and soaping.

Wetting, soaping and rubbing

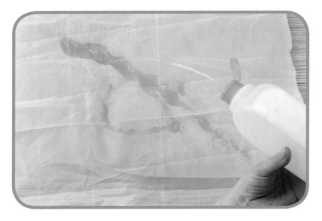

1 With the netting in position over the fleece, add a very small amount of washing-up liquid to an empty washing-up liquid bottle, just enough to cover the bottom, and then fill with warm water. Squeeze the soapy water onto the netting, as above, and be generous with it.

2 Once you have applied an ample amount of soapy water, you can begin to work the water through the fibre with a dishcloth. Hold the netting in place with one hand while you use the dishcloth to spread the water.

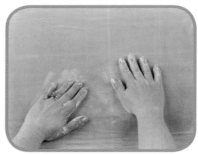

4 Once your fleece is flat and soapy, you can start to rub the soap in with your hands. Place your hands palm side down and keep them flat, fingers slightly parted. This will help you to maintain an even pressure. Rub using circular movements for approximately 10 minutes over the entire surface of the fleece.

3 Make sure that all of the fleece is flat with no lumpy bits of dry fleece. Now you can add the soap by adding a little water to the bar and getting it all nice and soapy in your hands, as shown above.

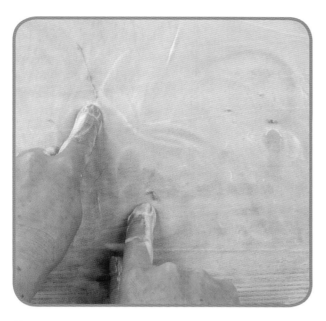 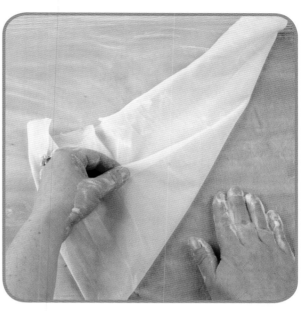

5 Make sure you check periodically for the first few minutes that the felt isn't becoming attached to the netting. You will know if this is happening as tiny little bits of wool will bobble through the netting; that is your signal to check.

6 Slowly pull the net back and gently detangle any stray bits. Once you have rubbed for about 10 minutes, turn the felt piece over, cover with the netting and rub the other side for around the same time.

7 You can use the S-test to check that your wool has felted properly. When you draw an S with your finger, the fibres should stay where they are. If they don't, you will need to carry on rubbing for a while.

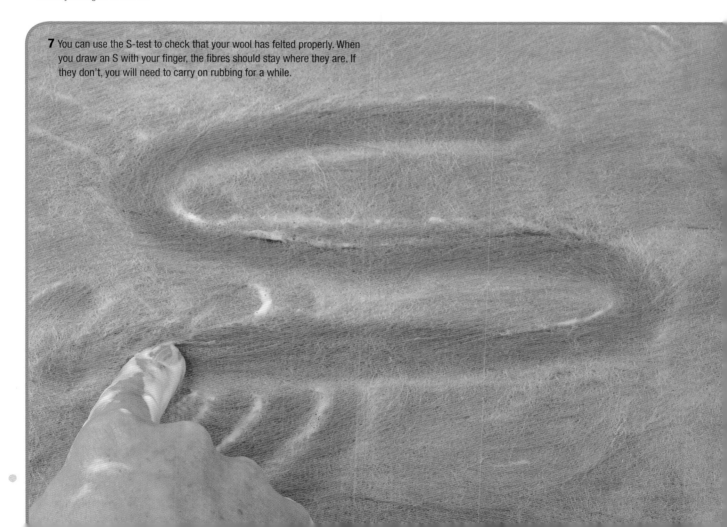

Rolling

**Once the merino is fully felted (when the fibres don't move about on firm touch)
you can start the rolling process.**

1 Turn the bamboo mat lengthways and tightly roll up the felt piece completely in the mat. Then roll it between
20 and 25 times in one direction, doing a full rotation back and forth.

2 Once you have completed this, unroll the felt and make
a quarter turn so that the felt is now sitting horizontally.
Tuck in the overhanging edges and repeat the rolling
sequence from step 1.

3 Unroll the felt and make another quarter turn so that the felt is now sitting vertically again and repeat the rolling sequence. Once you have completed this, unroll for the last time and make a quarter turn so that the felt is now sitting horizontally again. Tuck in the overhanging edges and repeat the rolling sequence. Once all four edges have been completed (top, bottom and either side of your felt piece), turn the felt over and repeat the entire rolling sequence again for the other side.

4 When you have completed all of the above on both sides, rinse the felt piece under very hot running water, followed by very cold water followed by very hot water; this will shock the felt and assist the felting process.

5 Take the felt piece back to the mat and give it a final rolling sequence on both sides and all four edges, but with far fewer rolls – so it could be up to 10 rolls per edge per side, or just a few depending on the shrinkage and the size you want to achieve.

6 Finally, rinse in warm water to remove all traces of soap, wring out the excess water and leave to dry on a radiator or a washing line.

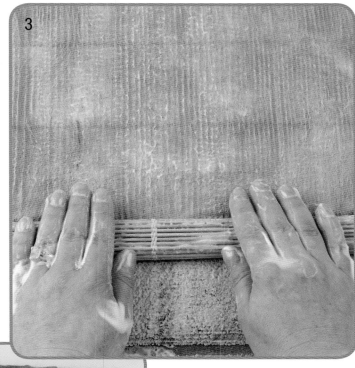

The finished and dried piece of felt. Press when dry.

Tip

If you want to make variegated felt, you can mix different colours by alternating the colours of the wisps of merino wool that you pull off at the start of the process and then using finer wisps in different shades of the same colour to lay over the top of that to blend them. See page 38 for more on making variegated felt.

Creating surface detail on flat felt

Surface detail is created by using very fine wisps of fibre and placing them onto the surface of the dry merino wool. You could just be making a flat piece of felt or creating a seamless project, such as a bag or a tea cosy. Whatever project you are creating, surface detail can be added.

The simplest form of surface embellishment is creating a swirl or circle for a dot. This is achieved by using very fine lengths of fleece. The general rule of thumb is, the longer the fine wisp is, the bigger the circle. Practise with some oddments of fibre before moving onto the main project itself.

1 First, pull off a wisp of merino that is a different colour from the main colour of your project or piece of flat felt.

2 Starting at the end of the wisp, tuck in the end and begin to gently coil the wisp. Keep this loose as you coil. If your wisp is too tightly coiled it may prove difficult to felt and not stay felted to your project. Coiling between your thumb and forefinger helps keep things in place, while your free hand acts as a guide.

3 Stop when it is the size you want or continue winding it round to use up the wisp of wool.

4 Position the circle on the base layer of merino wool.

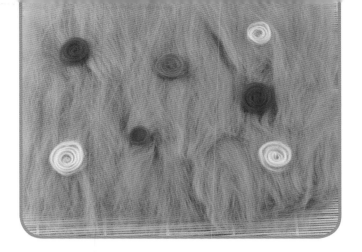

5 Make more circles in the colours of your choice, placing them carefully on the base layer. When you are happy with the position of the circles, you can start the wetting, soaping and rubbing process (see pages 18 and 19) but take great care not to dislodge them. If the circles do move a bit, pull back the netting and gently reposition them. Then follow the rolling process described on pages 20 and 21.

Alternatively, you may wish to make a surface pattern on the inside of your project. In the example below, I am using swirly shapes again and a plastic tea cosy template. See page 24 for more information on using a 'resist'.

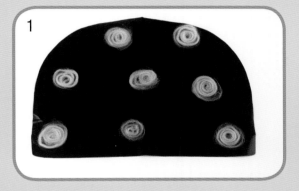

1 Begin by making circles as before with a different colour of merino wool from the main colour of your project. Position them where you wish on your plastic template.

2 Start pulling off wisps of merino in the main colour of the project and placing them horizontally on the plastic template, over the circle shapes.

3 Continue building up the wisps of wool in the main colour, taking care not to dislodge the circle shapes. Once this is done, start the wetting, soaping and rubbing process as described on pages 18 and 19.

As well as dots, you can make leaf and petal shapes and anything else you wish. The main thing to remember when adding decorative detail is to keep it fine. If you can see the main colour underneath, you can add finer wisps a bit at a time to get the desired effect. Remember that if the area is too thick with fleece it may not felt properly.

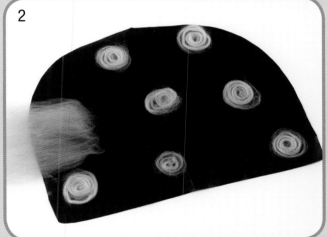

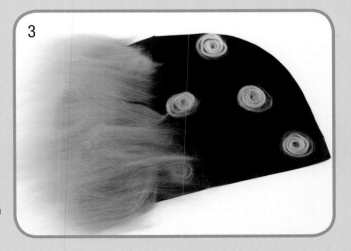

Working around a resist

A 'resist' is a plastic template that allows you to make a seamless item rather than a flat piece of felt. Here I am using a bag template to make a felted handbag (see page 60 for the rest of the project).

First of all, make your plastic template by copying the bag template (see the foldout sheet at the back of the book) onto paper and then transferring it to some plastic sheeting. Cut it out and you are ready to start.

Layer 1

1 Pull fine wisps from the merino fibre and lay them on the resist in a horizontal direction, overlapping the edges by about 1cm (½in). Make sure that the whole of the plastic template is covered.

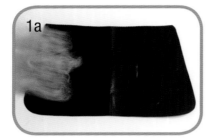
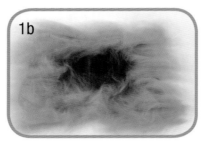
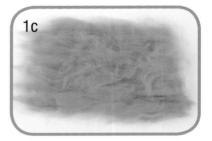

2 Place a piece of net over the top of the dry fleece then wet it with warm water with a splash of washing-up liquid in it. Take your dishcloth and work the water through the fleece until there are no air bubbles and the fleece is flat. Soap the top of the netting and your hands and rub for around 5–10 minutes.

3 Once you have been rubbing for a few minutes you may find that you get little bobbles of fleece coming through the net. When this happens, carefully peel back the net, detach the fibres, replace the net and continue rubbing. Use more soap if required.

4 Once you have rubbed for the appropriate amount of time, check that the fibre is felted enough; however, the fibre needs to have some movement remaining in it, in order for the next layer to felt to it, so don't felt it too much.

5 Try the S-test (see page 19), rubbing the felt with your finger from side to side. If the fibre moves a lot you need to rub more.

6 Now turn the resist over and tuck in the edges.

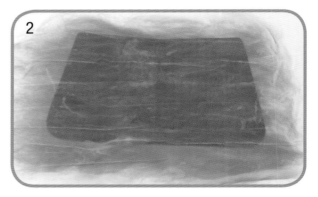

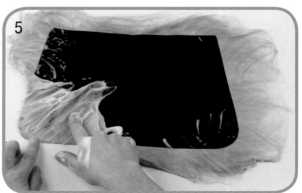

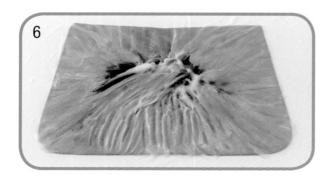

7 Begin to lay the wool over the edge of the plastic template on the side that you have just tucked in, as shown right, and cover the entire plastic template as you did with the first side. Wet, soap and rub as previously.

7a

7b

Layer 2

8 Lay wool over the side that you have just tucked in, but this time make sure that you lay the fleece in a vertical direction as shown below. Make sure that the entire shape is covered, not forgetting to leave an overhang of about 1cm (½in).

9 Cover with the netting, wet, soap and rub as with the first layer, turn your template over, tuck in the edges and lay a second vertical layer on the side that you have just tucked in. Cover, wet, soap and rub. So far you have done two sides horizontally and two sides vertically.

Layer 3

10 Place the final layer in a horizontal direction overlapping the edges (you may want to add a little extra here as this will be the last side that gets tucked in). Overlap all round the template by a width of about three fingers. Lay the netting over the fleece, then wet, soap and rub for 15–20 minutes or until felted (where the fibres don't move). Check periodically to ensure the fibre doesn't felt to the net.

11 Turn the template over, tuck in the edges and lay the fleece in the remaining space. Take care with this final layer, making sure you don't overfill the centre but fill enough to close the gap. The final layer doesn't need any overlap. Lay very fine wispy strands of fleece in different directions to hide any lines, then wet, soap and rub as before.

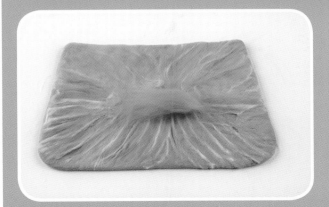

Rinsing and rolling

1 Gently rinse the felted bag in warm water and squeeze out the excess. Roll it tightly in the bamboo mat like a sausage, making sure that the whole project is covered by the mat. Roll it back and forth approximately 20 times, rotating it clockwise after each rolling session, so that top, bottom and side edges have been rolled. Turn the project over and repeat on the other side. See pages 20–21 for the rolling process.

2 Rinse it in very hot water, then cold water and then very hot again. Roll it again up to 10 times on all sides, or fewer if you want to control the size by doing a few rolls at a time.

Cutting and finishing

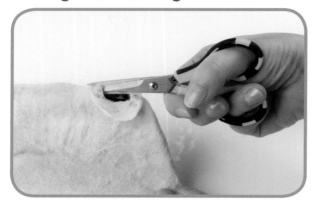

1 Cut a small incision at the top of the bag and gently cut through the layers, feeling your way to the plastic template. Be careful at this stage not to cut the plastic template itself.

2 Once you have cut a small hole through the layers, locate the plastic template with your fingers and push it to one side. Then cut a larger hole along the top of the bag to get the plastic template out.

4 To felt the raw edges, soak with soapy water, as shown below.

3 Once you have removed the plastic template, cut along towards the end of the bag and then trim off the top edges so it is level. Now you can decide if you want to overstitch the bag edges or felt the raw ends. If you decide to stitch the edges, go straight to step 6.

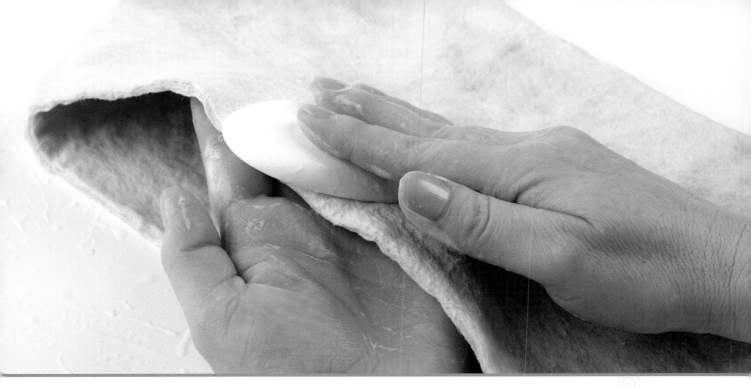

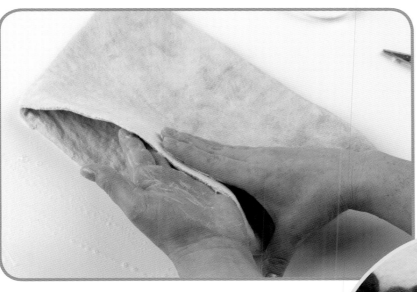

5 Using extra soap, rub the edges of the bag opening. Keep your fingers closed while felting. Use plenty of soap and rub with your fingers until the edges are completely felted.

6 Finally, thoroughly rinse all the soap out of the bag. It is important to get all the soap out. Make sure you get right inside the bag while rinsing and pay attention to the edges and corners where additional soap has been added. Leave to dry.

Tip

It is important to look at each individual project for extra tips on working around resists (plastic templates) with different shapes. For example, the peg bag (page 64), teapot (page 92) and teacups (page 88) are irregular shapes that will require some extra care and thought when laying the fleece.

Working around a resist with two layers

Some projects require only two layers of wool, otherwise the resulting felt would be too thick for the nature of the project. This is true of items such as the Rosalily Mobile Phone Case I am making here. You simply follow the steps for working around a resist on pages 24 and 25, but instead of three layers, you do only two.

Finished size

11 x 13cm (4½ x 5in)

What you need

For the case:

30–50g of merino
in sandstone
Plastic sheeting and template

For the embellishments:

10–15g of merino in salmon,
10g in pewter and small
amounts of various shades
of green
Leaf and scalloped
edge templates

Finishing:

Embroidery thread
Sewing needle
Hook and loop dots
Hot glue gun

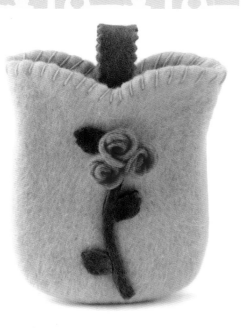

1 Apply a layer of sandstone merino horizontally onto the resist and follow the felting steps on page 24.

2 Turn the resist over and tuck in the edges.

3 Lay the merino horizontally for the back of the cover, then felt again. This completes the first layer.

4 Turn the resist, tuck in the edges, lay the wool vertically, and follow the felting steps.

5 Turn and tuck in the edges for the last time, then follow step 11 on page 25 to close the gap. This completes the second side. Follow the felting, rinsing and rolling steps (see pages 24–26) to finish the process.

Cutting and finishing

1 This is done freehand with scissors. Start at the right side and cut a curve into the centre, not too far down. To form the centre point, cut a curve to the left side. Once done, you can cut the rear of the phone case using the cut side as a guide.

2 Embroider the edges with an overstitch in matching embroidery thread. Start at the centre of either side as this will disguise the knot.

3 Make the flat felt for the roses and safety strap following the steps for wet felting on pages 16–21 and press when dry.

4 To make the felt for the leaves, lay the first layer of merino wool vertically instead of horizontally and use one shade of green. Place random shades of green over the top of this layer, in a horizontal direction. When this layer is added, add very fine wisps of different shades of green over the top to help blend the colours and eliminate a patchy finish. See the step-by-step photos on page 38 for making variegated felt.

5 Use any one of the scalloped templates you wish to create the roses. The roses in this project are four scallops in length but you can do more if you wish. Once the scalloped edge has been cut, narrow the straight edge substantially. Cut as close to the scallops as you can without weakening the finished edge. Roll and glue carefully as shown in the 'no-sew' rose instructions on pages 35 and 36.

6 Use the small leaf template (on the foldout sheet at the back of the book) to cut the leaves out of the green felt, or die cut them if you prefer. Cut a straight piece of green felt for the stem.

Fixing the embellishments

7 Fix the stem in place first, then the leaves on either side of the stem, using a hot glue gun. Place the roses and final leaf to see where you want them to sit and hot glue them in place. For the safety strap, cut a strip from the pewter felt approximately 1.5 x 7cm (½ x 2¾in) and cut around all four sides with pinking shears. Hot glue one side firmly to the inside back of the case and fix the other side with hook and loop dots.

Working around a 3D mould

Working around a polystyrene mould – a 'last' – is a great way to create form and shape that is functional, decorative and even wearable, such as the felt slippers on page 78. The principles are fundamentally the same, regardless of the shape you are creating.

 The main rule of thumb is to felt small, layered sections at a time. Each slipper is made up of three layers of fleece; that means that the sole, each side of the slipper and the top must have three layers. This will become clearer as we go through the process.

1 Cover each mould with a plastic food bag, tying the top of the bag with an elastic band, on the flat part of the top of the slipper. Cut off excess plastic above the elastic band. It is important that the bag is pulled tightly and secured with an elastic band. Any bits of bag sticking out need to be tightly taped down. The whole last should be sealed with no holes in the plastic at all. Then turn the last upside down and scrunch the towel up around it to stop it moving. Soak the bottom of the last (the sole) with warm soapy water.

2 Place wisps of felt vertically along the entire sole, making sure they are even and not too thick.

3 Then place wisps horizontally over the top of what you have just laid until the sole is covered.

Tip

If you have chosen a type of last that gives you a dual size option you will need to cut a few small air slits into the front as these can inflate and alter the slipper shape slightly.

4 Place the nylon netting over the top of the fleece and pull tightly to keep the wool in place.

5 Add a generous amount of soapy water and soap from your bar of soap and start rubbing. Use the palm of your hand to rub. You will need to rub each section for about 5–10 minutes, but in the first minute or two it is important to check for little bits of fibre that come through the netting and check that it isn't felting to the wool. Gently peel back the netting a bit at a time to detangle it from the wool. You may need to do this a few times per section in the first few minutes, and eventually it will stop coming through the netting.

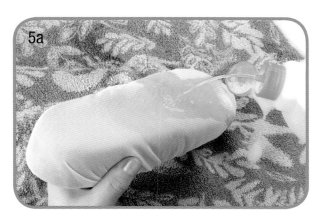

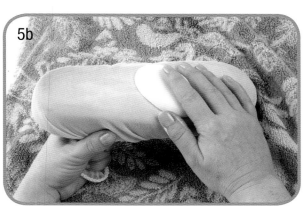

6 Work until each section is partially felted; this means that the felt feels firmer and doesn't move as much when you rub the raw fleece with your finger. However, you don't want it to be fully felted at this stage, otherwise it will be difficult to felt the next layer over it.

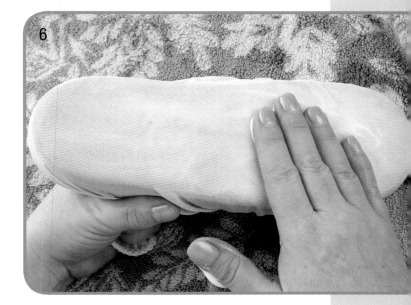

7 The next step is to turn the slipper last onto its side. Spray the last with soapy water.

8 Lay two even layers over each other, the first going horizontally ...

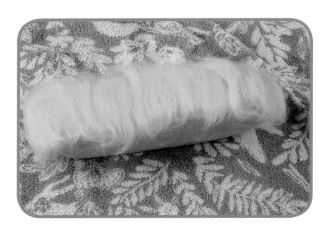

9 ... and the second one vertically over the top.

10 Cover with the netting, hold firmly in place and repeat steps 5 and 6 on page 31. Repeat the same sequence for the other side of the last and when you have done the sole and both sides, you will be ready to work on the top.

Tip

Once you have completed the first layer on last 1, do the first layer on last 2. This way you can keep track of progress and make sure that both lasts are evenly laid and felted, layer by layer.

For the slippers on page 78 I have used a slightly darker blue for the inside layer and the same colour for layers 2 and 3. However, you can choose to do three different colours to help you keep track of which layer you are on. A nice alternative for the middle layer would be the white felt used for the bow embellishment.

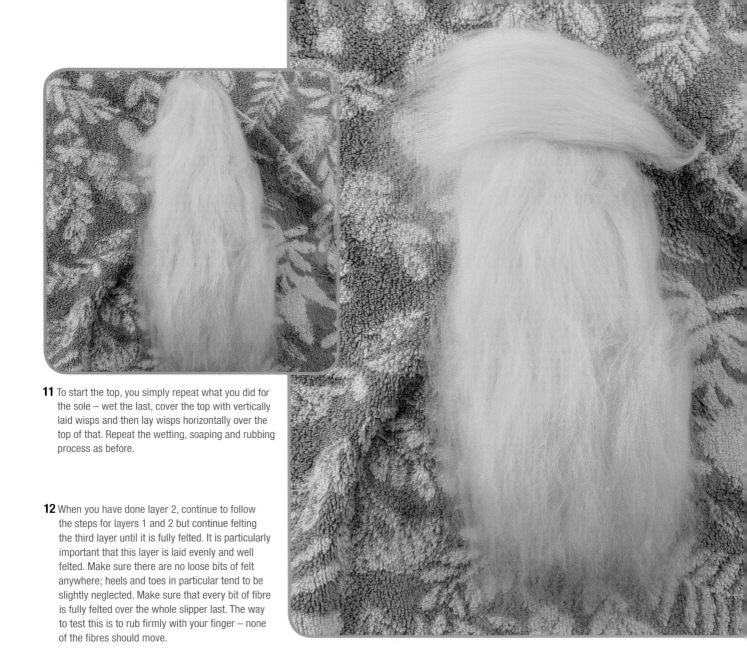

11 To start the top, you simply repeat what you did for the sole – wet the last, cover the top with vertically laid wisps and then lay wisps horizontally over the top of that. Repeat the wetting, soaping and rubbing process as before.

12 When you have done layer 2, continue to follow the steps for layers 1 and 2 but continue felting the third layer until it is fully felted. It is particularly important that this layer is laid evenly and well felted. Make sure there are no loose bits of felt anywhere; heels and toes in particular tend to be slightly neglected. Make sure that every bit of fibre is fully felted over the whole slipper last. The way to test this is to rub firmly with your finger – none of the fibres should move.

Machine washing

Once both lasts are covered and fully felted, they are ready for the next stage in the process. You will need a nylon net washing bag with a zip, the kind used to wash delicates in. Place both slippers in the bag. If you have already made the matching baby slippers, pop them into a separate wash bag. DON'T put the baby slippers in the same net washing bag. Wash the baby boy slippers separately as these are darker in colour and the colour may run into lighter colours if washed together. My top tip is to wash the same colours together. The machine should be set to a 60-degree wash cycle and only washing detergent or tablets should be used – no fabric softener and nothing else. Also, do not place towels or jeans in the machine – the only thing that should be in there is the slippers. Once they are washed and dried, you are ready for the next stage, which is cutting out. This is covered in the project chapter on page 78.

Felt embellishments

Felt flowers and leaves are a wonderful way of decorating your projects and giving them a finished and professional look. There are several ways of making them, all fun and easy!

How to make them

Felt flowers are made with pieces of flat felt (see page 16). Once you have a flat piece in your desired colour, you can create individual flowers in several different ways.

One way is to make individual petal shapes to build up the flower and create different types of flowers such as poppies, daffodils and daisies.

You can also use templates to cut out flower shapes, such as those included on the foldout sheet at the back of the book; or you can die cut them with a manual die-cutting machine and die.

There is no right or wrong way of creating flowers; it all comes down to what you want to achieve for each of your flower shapes and whether you want to stick to the project pattern, or go a little off-piste.

General flower shapes

The general flower shapes within this book have all been made with templates that you draw around and hand cut with a pair of sharp scissors. You can use these templates to create any number of different combinations and arrangements.

There's no reason why you can't use the templates to mix and match elements or even create new versions of the projects using different project elements from the different chapters. For example, you could add the scalloped bow on the slippers on page 78 to the bag on page 60. Once you're happy with the basic elements of felting, there will be no limit to the combinations you can create.

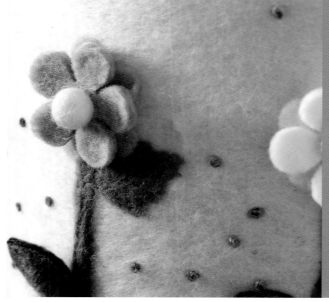

Making a 'no-sew' rose

A very popular flower for felted projects and accessories is the rose. The roses in this book can be created in a few different ways. To create a rose without a template or die, first of all establish what size you would like to make it and then cut out a square of felt. Once the size is established the process is the same, although if you are making very small roses, you might want to make the felt slightly thinner than other pieces – this will help obtain precision in the overall shaping.

Cutting

With all my roses, I round off the corners of the square of felt. This gives a realistic finished result and helps with the freehand shaping of the rose.

Tip

Before you start making your rose, practise with paper. Cut out differently sized squares and follow the steps below with paper to get a general idea of size. Felt is different and depending on how you assemble it, it may come out slightly smaller than the paper version. Further guidance on sizing will be found on the specific project pages with featured rose embellishments.

1 Start cutting the felt about 1cm (½in) away from the raw edge.

2 Making sure that you follow the rounded corners, continue to cut in a straight line.

3 Follow the shape of the square all the way into the centre, leaving a circle shape in the middle.

4 Starting from the beginning, cut a wavy or scalloped line following the outer edge of the felt.

5 As before, cut all the way into the centre of the rose, leaving a bit in the centre for the rose to sit on.

6 You can now start to assemble the rose. Using a hot glue gun, apply some glue to the end of the felt.

7 Start rolling the end of the felt into the glue, add another dab of glue and roll again.

8 You can see how the rose is beginning to take shape.

9 Take care to space the glue evenly so that the rose is not too tight or too loose and continue rolling it up towards the centre.

10 When you get to the centre, the circular flap of felt acts as a base for the rose to sit on. Add a final dab of glue…

11 … then push the flap down to stick it to the base of the rose.

The finished rose is ready to be applied to your project.

You could also make this rose by using the scalloped edge template included at the back of the book on the foldout sheet, or by using a die of your preference made with a die-cutting machine. The scalloped edge template is particularly useful for those who can't cut well freehand.

Tip

Although this rose is designed to be a 'no-sew rose', you can use felt glue or, alternatively, you can stitch the felt into place with a needle and thread if you don't want to use a hot glue gun.

Making leaves

First, you will need to make the felt for the leaves and this is done in a very similar way to flat felt. Refer to the laying of the fleece on pages 16 and 17, but instead of laying the first layer of fleece horizontally, lay it vertically. Then when you lay your second layer of fleece, you can blend different shades of green together for a more subtle and realistic effect. See page 38 for step-by-step instructions on how to do this.

Follow the remaining steps for making a flat piece of felt on pages 18–21 and leave to dry. Once the felt is dry, press it and use the leaf templates to cut out your leaf shapes; alternatively, you can die cut these with a die-cutting machine. See specific projects to see how you can use the leaves once they are cut.

Making variegated flat felt

 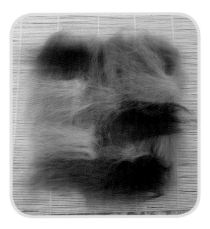 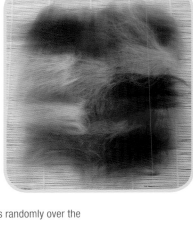

1 To make variegated flat felt for leaves, lay the first layer vertically instead of horizontally and use one shade of green.

2 Place wisps of green merino in different shades randomly over the top of this layer in a horizontal direction.

3 When this layer is complete, add very fine wisps of greens over the top to help blend the colours and eliminate a patchy finish.

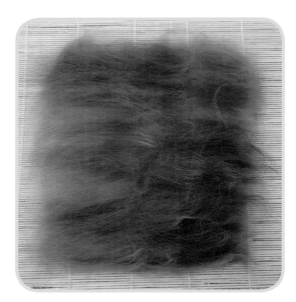

4 Continue to follow the steps for wet felting on pages 18–21 and when your finished felt is dry, press it well.

Making felt beads

1 To make beads for flower centres, wind a length of merino around your index finger and tuck the end inside the ball.

2 Wet the ball of merino thoroughly with soapy water.

3 Add plenty of soap from a bar, then roll the wool around the palms of your hands until it begins to felt. Add more soap if necessary, then roll it on your mat to firm it up and than back to your hands. Do this a few times until it feels really firm.

4 Finally, blast it with hot water from the kettle, then take it back to the mat for another roll and then blast with hot water again. Repeat the hot water followed by rolling a few times. Allow to cool, rinse the bead thoroughly and leave to dry.

The finished beads

Tip

To make flower bead centres, I recommend practising with different lengths and thicknesses of merino first, to work out your preferred size – felt making is not an exact science!

Needle felting

Needle felting is a process of matting and condensing woollen fibres together without the use of soap and water. It is sometimes called dry felting.

How does it work?

It works by using special felting needles that are commonly used in industrial felting. They are barbed, with indents or grooves along the shaft of the needle. These grooves pull the fibres downwards and tangle them with the lower layers of the fibres as the needle enters the wool. Because the barbs face downwards, they do not pull the fibres back out as the needle exits the wool. This in-and-out stabbing motion causes the wool fibres to mat together, gradually turning the wool into solid felt. In this way it is possible to create a whole host of surface enhancements and embellishments. The effects can be light or can be built up to create an almost embossed feel and finish.

Starting the process

The key to success is to use fine wisps of fleece to add surface pattern or enhance a pattern already created at the wet felt stage. The felting needle will need something to push against on the other side of the project, so a thick foam pad is placed underneath. Listen for the crunching sound it makes as it passes right through the project into the pad.

The fibre that is pulled through to the inside of the project will need to be periodically detangled from the foam mat, so that it doesn't felt to the mat. It's a similar process to checking that the project is not adhering to the netting in wet felting. It is worth getting a second mat to cut into smaller, more manageable pieces, to help get into awkward places (such as the toes in the slippers).

Creating shapes

To create the dots that are on the slippers on page 78, for example, you follow the same procedure as on page 22 for coiling the wool into your desired size.

The motion of needle felting doesn't require much force at all; it is a quick, light motion that pushes the needle through the embellishment and into the project itself in order to attach it. You can add additional shading and depth to the stem, leaf and flower areas of the Maisy Daisy Handbag (see page 60) as desired by placing wisps of fleece over the decorative areas. For the handbag, I chose not to embellish the flower shapes – only the stems, leaf areas and flower centres, as well as some spots for flower buds. Simply add fine wisps of fibre and push the needle in and out with a light, swift action.

1 Place a coil of merino onto the dry finished project and start to push the felting needle in and out to embed it to the surface of the felted project.

2 As you progress you will see the merino becoming more 'solid' and it will begin to look part of the surface, rather than standing proud of it.

3 If you can see the main colour through the dot, add more fine wisps to your shape. Check periodically that the project is not felting to the foam pad.

Your finished felted dot should be a neat circle like this, with no stray fibres poking out.

This is the reverse side of the work – you can see a fluffy 'halo' where the fibres have come through.

Needle felting solid shapes

Cutting out flower shapes and needle felting them to project surfaces is also a great way of adding embellishment.

1 Position your flower shape where you want it to sit on the project.

2 Begin needle felting and the flower will start to disappear into the surface.

3 When it is fully attached to the project, it will look flatter and less distinct.

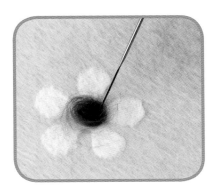

Tip

Take great care when needle felting and make sure you keep the needle as far away from your hands as possible to avoid injury.

4 Add a wisp of coiled merino and needle felt it into the centre and your flower is finished.

Embroidered embellishments

Embroidery is a great way to embellish finished felt items. It adds not only lustre but also texture, makes your projects look professional and provides you with a multitude of combinations that allow you to truly personalise your projects.

RUNNING STITCH

Running stitch forms a broken line. Bring the needle up at A, down at B, up again at C and so on to work running stitch.

BACKSTITCH

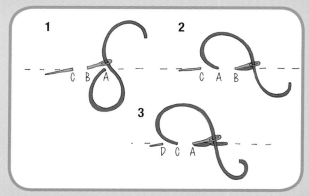

Backstitch forms a solid line. (1) Bring the needle up at A, then push it down at B, up again at C and pull it through. (2) Then take it down at B, and up at C to form your next stitch. (3) Repeat to form a line of stitches.

FRENCH KNOT

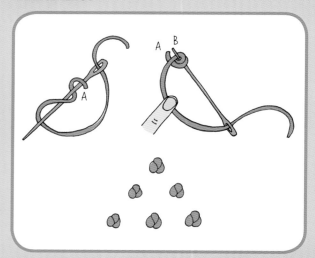

Bring the needle up at A, wind the embroidery thread around the needle twice (or three times for a more prominent knot) and hold the loops while you take the needle down at B.

CROSS STITCH

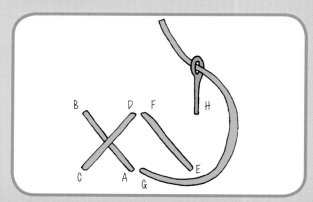

Bring the needle up at A, take it diagonally across and down at B, then up at C and down again at D. This forms your first cross. Continue the same pattern to make more crosses.

CHAIN STITCH

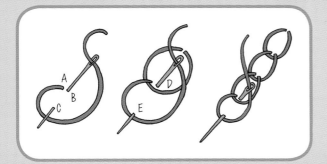

Chain stitch forms a line of chains. Bring the needle up at A, then down at B (very close to where you came up at A), then up at C, looping the thread under the needle, and pull it through to form the first chain. Take the needle down at D (just inside the first chain), then up at E to form the next stitch, and so on.

LONG STITCH

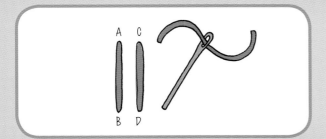

Long stitch is worked vertically. Bring the needle up at A, take it down at B, then up at C and down again at D. The stitches do not have to be the same length – just make sure you don't make them too long.

OVERSTITCH

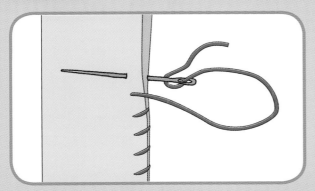

Overstitch can be used to join two pieces of felt together, or to neaten an unfelted edge. Knot the embroidery thread, bring it up through both layers of felt from back to front, then make the next stitch the same way, a little distance from the original stitch. Be sure to space the stitches evenly for a neat finish.

LAZY DAISY STITCH

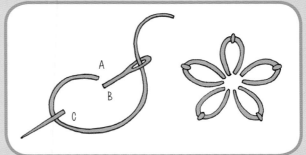

Lazy daisy stitch is basically chain stitch in the form of a daisy. Bring the needle up at A, then push it down at B, up again at C and pull it through. Then take the needle down close to the first complete stitch and repeat to make the next petal, and so on.

HERRINGBONE STITCH

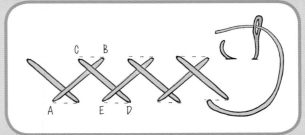

Working from left to right, bring the needle up through the fabric at A and work a stitch diagonally to the upper right (B). Bring the needle up again at C (to the left of B), and then work a stitch diagonally to the lower right (D). Come back up to the left of this at E, and repeat the pattern, making as many stitches as you wish.

SATIN STITCH

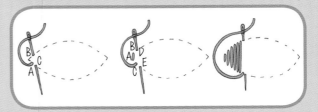

Satin stitch is a great stitch for filling in shapes such as leaves or petals. Bring the needle up from the back of your work at A, then down at B and up again next to A, at C. Take it back to D (close to B) and up again at E. Continue making parallel stitches like this until you have filled the shape.

The projects

Finished size

12 x 11cm (4½ x 4in)

What you need

For the main case:

20–30g of merino in cerulean
for the house (or 15 x 24cm/
6 x 9½in of pre-felt), 10–15g
in spearmint for the door and
windows (or 6 x 8cm/2¼ x 3in
of pre-felt), 10–20g in teal for
the roof (or 13 x 15cm/5 x 6in
of pre-felt) and 10g in aqua
for the rose (or 5 x 12cm/
2 x 4¾in of pre-felt)

A fat quarter or a 20 x 29cm
(8 x 11½in) offcut of fabric

An offcut of mint green felt for
the needle holder

Short length of ribbon

Paper templates

Ballpoint pen

Finishing:

Embroidery thread

Sewing needle

Flat-back pearl (optional)

Hook and loop dots

Hot glue gun

Make the flat felt for the sewing case
following the steps on pages 16–21 and
press when dry. Try making two colours at a
time by laying the fibres next to each other on
the bamboo mat. I have suggested generous
quantities of merino, as you may use more
when you are learning to felt. Leftover pieces
can be used for other projects.

Using the templates on the foldout sheet,
use a ballpoint pen to draw around them
on the felt and cut out the pieces. The pen
marks will not be seen, as they will be on the
inside. You can use a combination of machine
stitching and hand stitching, or just hand
stitching. I used a combination. Fold the main
piece of felt for the cottage in half and press
a fold in it. This will act as a marker from
where to start your stitching. The door can
either be rectangular (see opposite) or arched,
as in the step-by-step photographs. Both are
included in the templates.

Snowdrop Cottage Sewing Case

Make a lovely sewing case for yourself or as
a gift for someone special.

1 Position the door in the middle of the felt,
sitting on your halfway fold, and machine
stitch it in place using four evenly spaced,
vertical lines.

2 Place a window either side of the door
and stitch a vertical and horizontal line on
both to represent window panes.

3 Embroider a French knot
for the door handle (I
triple wrapped the knot to
make it more prominent)
and more French knots
and herringbone stitch
around the outside of
the cottage windows
to represent stems and
flowers (see pages 42
and 43).

4 Cut a piece of lining fabric using the template to match the outer piece of the cottage. To make the needle holder, cut a piece of mint green felt into a rectangle. This can be as big or as small as you like, although I would recommend keeping a border of fabric around it. Finish the edges of the felt with pinking shears to minimise fraying. Fold it in half and pin it in the centre of the fabric lining.

5 Sew the felt across the centre.

6 With right sides together, pin the fabric to the felt.

7 Machine stitch the bottom and sides. Make sure you start at the opposite end to the door and windows. This will then leave an opening in the right place. If you don't have a sewing machine, you will need to work with right sides facing out and press the raw edges under before stitching. Use ladder stitch or a similar stitch so that the stitching will be invisible.

8 Turn the piece through to the right side, using the open top end to push the corners out.

9 Cut out a short piece of ribbon to make a tab. Fold the roof in half and cut a slit into the felt where the ribbon will go. Fold the ribbon in half and slide it through the slit. Tuck in and press the raw edges of the open end of the case.

10 Place the cottage onto the WS of the roof, aligning the pressed edges with the halfway fold. Tuck the ribbon into the pressed open end and stitch across the length of the pressed edges, closing the edges and securing the ribbon in place. The roof can now be folded over the front of the cottage. Topstitch the bottom edge of the cottage if you wish.

11 Add hook and loop dots to fasten – one on the underside of the roof and one to correspond on the front above the cottage door. Finish by gluing a flower embellishment of your choice to the roof with a flat-back pearl in the centre.

Mary Anna's Pincushion

This attractive and handy pincushion can be made as just one or as a stack, making your sewing chores an absolute dream.

Finished size

14 x 14cm (5 x 5in); cushion stack 19cm (7in)

What you need

For the pincushion stack:

15–30g of merino in each of aqua, spearmint, teal, peppermint and mallard green

Small amounts of co-ordinating pre-felt

Hot glue gun or fabric glue

A small amount of toy stuffing

For the decorative detail:

White/natural pre-felt

Pompom trim in mint green (approximately 40cm/15¾in long for a small pincushion)

Satin piping trim in teal (approximately 40cm/15¾in long for a small pincushion)

Scraps of pre-felt for centre back detail

Paper templates for flowers and hearts

Finishing:

A button of your choice

Embroidery thread

Long sewing needle

An example of a single pincushion with a pompom trim.

1 Follow the steps for making flat felt on pages 16–21 (and see Tip, right). Cut two pieces of aqua felt to 9 x 9cm (3½ x 3½in), two pieces of spearmint felt to 10 x 10cm (4 x 4in), two pieces of teal felt to 11.5 x 11.5cm (4½ x 4½in), two pieces of peppermint felt to 13 x 13cm (5 x 5in) and two pieces of mallard green felt to 15 x 15cm (6 x 6in).

2 Using white or natural pre-felt, cut out flower shapes, heart shapes and dots using either the templates on the foldout sheet or a die-cutting machine if you prefer.

3 Use the needle felting techniques as described in the needle embellishments section on pages 40 and 41. Apply flowers, hearts and dots as you wish to one piece of each colour. You won't need to embellish the bottom squares as very little of this will be visible.

4 For cushions without a trim, place right sides together and stitch a seam of approximately 5mm (¼in) around all four sides. Cut a slit in the centre back piece (see step 9 on page 52) and then continue with step 12 onwards to finish the cushion.

Tip

You will need five different colours of felt and enough to make two squares for each cushion. I recommend that you make two colours at a time by laying the fibres next to each other; lay one colour horizontally, then lay the next colour horizontally next to that. Then repeat each colour with the fibres laid vertically. The pincushion is made up of five differently sized cushions in different colours. Press each felt piece before use, as it makes it more condensed, looks neater and is easier to work with.

5 For cushions with a trim, pin the edging trim (or satin piping) to the right side of the square. The trim part should be facing in the direction of the cushion centre, on the embellished side. Place this all the way round the four sides, pinning as you go.

6 You will need to bend and stretch the trim into place at the corners and cross the ends over, leaving some overlap where the two ends meet.

7 Sew the side where the raw edge is exposed, but keep as close to the start of the edging as you can.

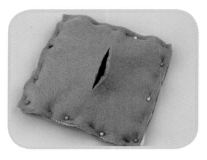

8 When you reach the corner where the trim overlaps, take the machine back and forth to secure the thread.

9 Cut a slit into the centre of the second piece of the cushion that is big enough to get the stuffing in and to turn inside out after sewing.

10 Place the bottom part of the cushion over the top part, right sides facing, and pin all round.

11 Sew the two pieces together, trying to keep the stitching in the same place as the stitched trim.

12 Turn right sides out, check that the corners are *in situ* and the overlapped trim ends have matched well, leaving no gaps in the edging. Turn back to the wrong side and trim off the excess seam allowance.

13 Turn back the right way and stuff the cushion with toy stuffing until you are happy with the shape.

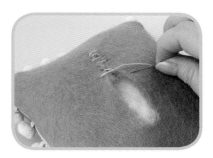

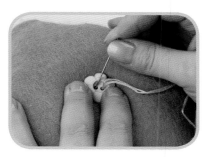

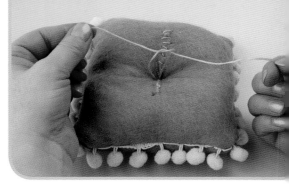

14 Now hand stitch the opening closed – it doesn't have to be particularly neat as this will be covered with the piece of pre-felt.

15 With your embroidery thread held double, attach the button embellishment to the front of the cushion by taking the needle right through from the back of the cushion to the front. You only need to add a button to the top cushion if you are making the stack.

16 Tie a knot at the back of the cushion and then snip off the excess embroidery thread.

17 Fix a piece of pre-felt to the bottom of each cushion you make, except for the very bottom one, which needs to remain uncovered until you have sewn all five together. Make the other four in the same way.

Tip

If you prefer to hand stitch the pincushion stack, cut each piece of felt 1cm (½in) bigger to allow for folding in and pressing seams. Use ladder stitch or another invisible stitch to sew the seams. The trim will be visible and sewn on the outside if you are hand stitching.

Fixing the stack together

To fix the whole stack of pincushions together, use a long needle and double embroidery thread. Enter at the centre back of the first and largest cushion, come through the top of that cushion into the bottom of the next cushion and so on, until you come through the fifth and final cushion. Push the needle through the buttonhole into the other side and back down through all five cushions, pulling tightly when you get to the other end. Continue to sew up and down the cushions through the button a couple more times, then pull tightly and knot. Finish by sewing a piece of pre-felt on the bottom cushion to hide the stitches.

Finished size

12 x 12cm (4½ x 4½in)

What you need

- 20–30g of merino in amethyst and 10–15g each in lightning and lilac
- Plastic sheeting and template
- Bubble wrap
- Paper templates for flower, heart and scalloped trim

Finishing:
- Embroidery thread
- Sewing needle
- Hot glue gun

Queen of Hearts Egg Cosy

This stylish and quirky egg cosy will make a fine job of keeping your morning egg nice and warm. You will need to work around a 'resist' or plastic template to make this project.

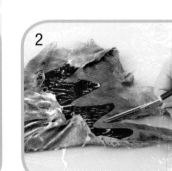

1 This is a two-layer project, so follow the steps for working around a resist on pages 28 and 29. However, before you lay the horizontal fibres, lay fine wisps vertically between the prongs. Cover the resist with fibres, then wet felt.

2 When you turn the plastic template over to tuck in the sides, cut the wet felt in between the prongs to enable you to fold it in. Don't cut too close to the plastic template.

3 It is very important to tuck the edges around the plastic template neatly and tightly. Because of the unique shape, be sure to cover the edges of the plastic template generously.

4 Follow the remaining steps for working around a resist on pages 28 and 29, laying wool vertically between the prongs and felting until your project is completed, then cut the bottom edge of the crown and remove the plastic template.

5 Once cut and trimmed, size the cosy by continuing to roll and shrink it in the bamboo mat, reshaping in between. Test the size periodically over an egg in an egg cup. Shape the cosy by adding more soap and water. Push the round end of an old dried-up pen or similar up into each prong to help provide more shape and dimension. Add soapy water and soap and rub thoroughly around the crown and prongs. Make sure the cosy is very soapy and moist to prevent the wool from bobbling.

6 When fully shaped, rinse the soap out completely with a combination of warm and cold water. Fill the prongs and cosy with bubble wrap to help keep its shape and leave to dry on a towel over a radiator.

7 Make the flat felt for the heart and white scalloped trim by following the steps on pages 16–21. Press when dry. Make four small beads by following the steps on page 39.

8 Cut out the heart using the template and finish with an embellishment of your choice. I used a die-cut flower and needle-felted the centre to secure it to the heart.

9 Use the scalloped edge template for the trim and overstitch it to the crown with embroidery thread (see page 43). Finally, glue the heart and felted beads in place.

Finished size

11 x 13cm (4½ x 5in)

What you need

20–30g of merino in cerulean, 10–15g each in lightning and various shades of green and a small amount in peppermint
Plastic sheeting and template
Bubble wrap

For the decorative detail:
16cm (6¼in) length of charcoal polka dot ribbon
Mini playing cards

For the flower detail:
Small amount of white pre-felt
Small pale blue felt bead
Paper templates for flower, scallop and leaf

Finishing:
Embroidery thread
Sewing needle
Hot glue gun

Mad as a Hatter Egg Cosy

Impress your overnight guests at breakfast with this stylish and fun hatter-style egg cosy. This project uses a 'resist' or plastic template.

1 This cosy is a two-layer project, so follow the steps for working around a resist on pages 28 and 29. As with the crown egg cosy, you will need to pay attention to the edges of the plastic template and make sure they are generously covered.

2 Cut the bottom edge of the hat and remove the template.

3 Trim the bottom edge so that it is even. Test the size periodically over an egg in an egg cup. When you have achieved the desired size, you can begin shaping the brim of the hat.

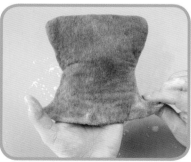

4 To shape the hat, bend the bottom up and start flattening it out. To start with you will have a little dimple either side of the hat rim where the template was. This can be easily smoothed by adding plenty of soap and soapy water.

5 Continue to felt the brim with your hands, shaping it as you go.

6 When you have shaped the brim of the hat, you may need to trim it a little.

7 Shape the top of the hat by adding more soapy water and soap, while pulling, bending and felting it to the desired shape.

8 Make sure that both points of the hat are symmetrical. Get your hand in the hat to shape the inside.

9 Once you are happy with the shape, follow the steps for rinsing and insert bubble wrap as you did for the crown cosy. Leave it to dry.

10 Work overstitch round the edge of the brim to give it a nice finish (see page 43).

11 Cut out a rose using one of the scallop templates and make a 'no-sew' rose following the instructions on pages 35 and 36. Then make a stem for the flower and some leaves. For the stem, follow the steps for making a felt handle on page 62, but use much shorter, finer lengths of wool.

12 To make felt for the leaves, follow the steps on page 38, then continue with the wet felting instructions on pages 18–21. Use the small leaf template to cut out two leaves.

13 Fix the stem by poking a hole into the top of the hat on one side, pushing the stem through and gluing it to the inside of the cosy.

14 Finish by gluing a charcoal polka dot ribbon just above the brim and add mini playing cards. Cut a small flower out of pre-felt and glue it to the rear to help fix the ribbon (see photograph opposite, bottom left). Make a tiny felt bead (see page 39) and glue it to the centre of the pre-felt flower.

'Time for Tea' Tea Cosy

It's always time for tea in our house. The best kind of time is when friends and family arrive for afternoon tea and it absolutely has to be served in fine bone china cups. To make this tea cosy you need to work around a 'resist' or plastic template.

1 The tea cosy is made with two layers of felt rather than three, so follow the steps for working around a resist with two layers on page 28. You will need to add the decorative surface detail to the front side of the last layer (the back is not as suitable as this will be where you fill in the 'gap').

2 To add the surface detail, use white/natural and coral pre-felt, and the flower templates to cut out the flower shapes. If you prefer, you can die cut the flowers. Place the netting over the surface detail, wet with soapy water and press your dishcloth into the surface pattern, making sure that the whole surface area is fully wet and pressed – this will reduce movement in the surface pattern. Continue to work the water through the top layer of wool. Add soap and continue to felt. Check regularly for the first 5 minutes to make sure the netting isn't felting to the wool and to check any movement of the pattern, which you can quickly rectify. Continue with the rest of the steps for working around a resist on pages 28 and 29.

3 Follow the cutting and finishing steps on page 26 to release the plastic template from the felt and leave the cosy to dry. I have used overstitch (see page 43) all the way round the bottom of the cosy, so it's not necessary to felt the raw edges.

4 When the cosy is dry, needle felt the flower centres in a different colour to the petals (see pages 40 and 41 for needle felting).

5 Make the flat felt for the 3D flowers following the steps on pages 16–21 and press the felt when dry. Make the felt beads for the flower centres following the steps on page 39.

6 Make the flat felt for the leaves following the steps on page 38 and press the felt when dry.

7 Use the flower and leaf templates on the foldout sheet to cut out your desired combination of flowers and leaves, using an erasable marker pen to draw around the templates. Alternatively, you can die cut the flowers on a machine. Remove the pen lines with water. Stitch veins along the leaves either by machine or by hand.

8 Do a practice layout with the cosy laid flat and decide where you want your flowers and leaves to go.

9 Fix them in place with a dab of glue from a hot glue gun.

Finished size

25 x 33cm (10 x 13in)

What you need

For the cosy:
   100g of merino in peach

For the flowers:
   20–30g each of merino in minky taupe, flesh and salmon
   Plastic sheeting and template
   Hot glue gun

For the leaves:
   20–30g of merino in each of olive, mid olive, green grass and pale olive

For the needle-felted flowers:
   Small amounts of pre-felt in salmon and white/natural
   Paper templates for flowers and leaves

Finishing:
   Small amounts of leftover wool from the tea cosy and flowers can be used for the flower centre beads
   Embroidery threads
   Sewing needle

Examples of flower embellishments you can make for the tea cosy.

Maisy Daisy Handbag

This is a beautiful yet very practical project. To make it, you need to work around a 'resist' or plastic template.

Finished size

16 x 26cm (7 x 10in)

What you need

For the main bag:
  100g of merino in aqua
  Plastic sheeting and template
  Hot glue gun

For the flower surface detail:
  Small amounts of pre-felt in salmon, flesh, lavender, damson and grass

For the 3D flower embellishments:
  20–30g of merino in orchid, lavender and hyacinth (approximately 20 x 22cm/8 x 8¾in)
  Paper templates for flowers

For the felt handles:
  Two equal lengths (approximately 60cm/23½in) of merino in heather

For needle embellishing:
  Small amounts of merino in olive, mid olive, green grass, pale olive, aubergine, heather, flesh and sandstone

For the bead flower centres:
  Small amounts of merino in grass or chartreuse

For the remaining flower centres:
  Flat-back pearls
  Silver rim pearls
  Wooden flower embellishments

Finishing:
  Embroidery thread
  Sewing needle

1 Follow the steps for working around a resist on pages 24–27. Add the decorative surface detail to the front side of the last layer (the back is not as suitable as this will be where you fill in the 'gap'). To do this, use grass, flesh, salmon, lavender and damson pre-felt. Cut out wavy or straight stems as you prefer. Use the leaf template to cut out the leaves. Use the flower templates to cut out a selection of different coloured flowers. For the sprig of lavender, make small circles by following the steps on page 22. Place the stems and leaves first and then the flowers and lavender (see photograph below).

2 Place the netting over the surface detail, wet with soapy water and press your dishcloth into the surface pattern, making sure that the whole surface area is fully wet and pressed. This will reduce any movement in your surface pattern. Continue to work the water through the top layer as in step 2 on page 18. Add soap and continue to felt. Check regularly for the first 5 minutes to make sure the netting isn't felting to the wool and to check any movement of the pattern, which you can quickly rectify. Continue with the rest of the steps for working around a resist on pages 25–27.

3 When the bag is dry, use fine wisps of fibre to needle felt the flower centres and to add further dimension and decorative detail to the surface pattern and lavender on the front of the bag. You can use a mix of green shades of merino to add variation to the stems and leaves. Add running stitch, backstitch or chain stitch as desired to the stems and leaves. See the stitch diagrams on pages 42 and 43.

4 Make the flat felt for the flower embellishments following the steps on pages 16–21 and press the felt when dry. To make the felt for the leaves, follow the steps on page 38.

5 Use the flower templates or a die-cutting machine to cut out your desired combination of flowers, and make felt bead centres by following the steps on page 39.

The felt stems, flowers and leaves in position on the front side of the last layer before felting.

Making felt handles

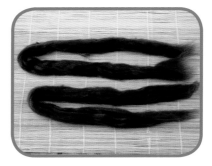  

6 To make the handles, choose the length of heather merino you want, making sure they are equal.

7 Wind each one into a rough ball to make it easier to wet.

8 Add warm water with a few drops of washing-up liquid added and soak the wool thoroughly.

9 Work the liquid through the handles and cover with soap all the way along the length. Make sure the wool is thoroughly wet and soaped as this will help keep it smooth. Fold the bamboo mat over the top and roll back and forth, moving the cords up and down the mat periodically. Keep adding soap and water and roll until the cord feels firm. Pour boiling water over the cord, leave to cool and then continue soaping and rolling, repeat the boiling water two or three times, rolling in between.

10 The handles will be very soapy so rinse them really thoroughly until the water runs clear.

11 It is best to attach the handles when they are still wet and you can attach them to a wet bag too if you wish. Lay out the handles and position them where you want them to sit. Use the sharp end of your scissors to poke two holes through both the front and back of your bag, evenly spaced. Take one handle end and push it through the first hole in the front of the bag, pushing it from the inside of the bag to the outside with the scissors. Repeat for the second end. Then pull the back handle through in the same way. Measure how long or short you want them to be. Once you are happy with the length, tie the ends in a knot. At this point you can choose to leave the ends dangling as a feature or glue them out of view around the knot itself.

12 When the bag and handles are fully dry, embroider some star shapes between the flowers and some veins and shading on the leaves and stems.

13 Fix the bead centres to the larger flowers and pearls or centre embellishments of choice for the smaller flowers. I chose some wooden shapes, which I painted and then added a flat-back pearl. Do a practice layout with the bag laid flat and decide where you want your flowers to go. This project has bigger flowers in the centre and smaller ones at the outer edges. Fix them into place using a hot glue gun.

Alice Peg Bag

This peg bag will evoke an air of nostalgia and memories of past times. Team it up with painted wooden dolly pegs for a truly vintage look – the prettiest accessory to adorn your washing line. This project is worked around a 'resist' or plastic template.

Finished size

35 x 37cm (13 x 15in)

What you need

For the main bag:

100g of merino in flesh
Plastic sheeting and template
Ballpoint pen and ruler

For the apron and embellishments:

50–100g of merino in white
Paper templates

For the embroidery:

Embroidery hoop
Paper template
Water-soluble fabric
Embroidery threads in shades of coral and green
Sewing needle

Finishing:

Small amount of pre-felt flower embellishments in flesh
Paper template for flowers
Child's wooden coat hanger measuring up to 30cm (11¾in)
Hot glue gun
Silver rim pearls

Flat felt sizes:

Dry unfelted fleece for top half of apron when laid should measure approximately 40½ x 51cm (16 x 20in); when felted, 33 x 38cm (13 x 15in)
Dry unfelted fleece for bottom half should be laid to similar proportions for the top apron; when felted, approximately 33 x 35.5cm (13 x 14in)

This is a two-layer project. Follow the steps for working around a resist on page 28. For this project, you remove the plastic template in a different way from previous projects, by making a square hole in the back and pulling it through.

1 Begin by laying fine wisps of merino around the shaped areas of the plastic template, pointing towards the centre. Do this before you do the horizontal and vertical layers.

2 Felt following the steps on page 28, but before you finish the last layer you will need to add the decorative surface detail to the right side. Use fine wisps of white merino wool to create swirls, as shown on page 22.

3 Once you have placed the surface detail, continue with the wet felting process, taking care not to dislodge the swirls. Check regularly for the first 5 minutes to make sure the netting isn't felting to the wool and to check any movement of the pattern, which you can quickly rectify. Continue with the rest of the steps for working around a resist on page 28, but be careful of too much shrinkage at this stage; use the coat hanger as a guide to shrinkage and make sure you have room on either side of the sleeves.

4 Once your peg bag is felted to size, you need to remove the plastic template by cutting a square hole in the back. First of all, measure near the top to find the centre and mark it with a ballpoint pen. Measure about 4.5cm (1¾in) out on either side and mark, and do the same top and bottom so you have marked out a square.

5 Starting off in the centre, make a small slit and then cut diagonally to a mark at the top. Repeat the diagonal cuts until it looks like the photograph above, then cut away the excess triangles of felt so you are left with a square hole.

6 You should now be able to remove the plastic template from the peg bag.

7 You can then make the square peg opening. It needs to be big enough to get the coat hanger in, but not so big that you lose form and structure. Cut a bit at a time using your ruler for guidance.

8 Poke a small hole in the centre top of the peg bag with the pointed end of your scissors. Insert the coat hanger at this stage while the felt is still damp as it will be easier to get in. You may have to put one end in first and then ease the other end in.

9 Make the flat felt for the apron following the steps on pages 16–21 and press when dry.

10 Use the templates to cut out the different felt parts of the apron. You will need to measure the width of the waistband to see how much felt you need for the central scalloped strip.

Tip

I recommend using a hot glue gun to attach the various apron pieces and bows (see right) to the peg bag. Felt is a non-woven fabric and stitching can work itself loose as a result.

11 To make the embroidered motif, first you need to transfer the embroidery design onto the water-soluble fabric. To do this, place the printed motif under the soluble fabric, which is semi-transparent, and trace the design onto it with a ballpoint pen.

12 Pin the fabric to the top part of the apron. Using a small embroidery hoop to hold the design in place and starting in the centre, embroider the rose and leaves in shades of coral and green embroidery thread using satin stitch (see page 43). When complete, remove from the hoop and cut away as much of the excess soluble fabric as you can. Then run the motif on the apron under warm water to dissolve the excess fabric. Leave to dry.

13 To finish the peg access hole, use a spare piece of felt from the apron that is big enough to cover the hole and leave excess for the scalloped edging. Feel for the four corners and mark the felt. Draw a straight line between each of the four marks and cut out the square.

14 Now use the scalloped template to mark the edge around the remaining felt edges. Cut it out, pin it over the hole in the apron back and overstitch the two layers together with embroidery thread to match the apron body.

Use painted dolly pegs to complete the vintage look of the peg bag.

15 Fix the top and bottom parts of the apron using a hot glue gun. Dab a dot of glue under each shoulder and along the bottom edge of the apron top. Run a line of glue along the straight edge of the bottom part of the apron. Fix the scalloped waistband a little at a time with small dabs of glue.

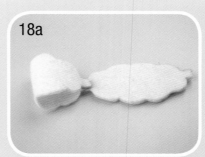

16 Using the bow templates, cut out a medium bow for the back and a small bow for the front.

17 To assemble the bows, glue one tab of one bow part onto the tab of the other.

18 Then each remaining tab end of each part can be folded over into the centre and glued in place.

19 Use the central band piece to wrap around the middle of the bow to hold and hide the joins.

20 Fix the medium bow over the join of the apron waistband at the back with hot glue and the small bow to cover up the small hole in the top where the hanger goes.

21 Complete the waistband by gluing on three evenly spaced flowers with a flat-back pearl in the centre of each.

Tigerlily Lampshade

This wonderfully practical lampshade will be a feature in any room. Alice talks to a flower called Tigerlily, giving this flower-themed project the perfect nod to Wonderland.

A basic lampshade kit consists of two lampshade rings (one with a central bulb fitting), a self-adhesive lampshade panel, a roll of double-sided sticky tape and a set of instructions. This is the easiest way to make a lampshade. Simply measure the self-adhesive lampshade panel and this gives you the approximate size of the piece of felt that you need to make.

Tip

Buy your lampshade kit first and measure the circumference of the lamp rings – then you will know how much felt you need to make!

1 Make the flat felt for the 3D flowers following the steps on pages 16–21 and press when finished. Make variegated felt for the leaves following the steps on page 38. Use the flower and leaf templates to cut out your desired combination of flowers and leaves, or die cut them with a die-cutting machine if you prefer.

2 Make a piece of flat felt for the lampshade measuring approximately 27 x 71cm (10¾ x 28in). If your lampshade kit is a different size from mine, bear in mind that the felt needs to be a bit larger than the self-adhesive panel that comes in your lampshade kit. Press when finished.

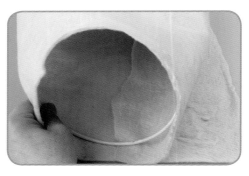

3 Wrap the dry felt round the lampshade ring to measure it.

4 Cut the felt to the size of the lampshade ring leaving a 1.5cm (½in) overhang.

Finished size

Dependent on your lampshade kit; my lampshade was 22cm high x 66cm in circumference (8¾in high x 26in in circumference)

What you need

For the flat felt:

100–200g of merino in peppermint

Paper template for scalloped edge

For the 3D flower embellishments:

10–20g of merino in minky taupe, lilac, lightning, orchid and aubergine

Small amounts of pre-felt in green for the stems/leaves

Paper templates for flowers and leaves

For the needle embellishment:

Small amounts of merino in various shades of green

For the needle-felted flowers:

Small amounts of pre-felt in white, lilac and purple

For the leaves, use leftover felt from other leaf projects or create more (see page 38)

For the bead centres:

Leftover merino of choice

Finishing:

Embroidery thread

Sewing needle

A lampshade kit for a table lamp or lamp-making accessories (see introduction above)

Table lamp base

Hot glue gun

5 Use the scalloped template in the book to create a scalloped edge, remembering to measure enough overhang so that the edging doesn't expose the ring and leaving enough at the top edge to be tucked over the top lamp ring.

6 To add the decorative detail, use green pre-felt and cut wavy or straight stems as you wish. Cut the flowers and leaves using the templates. If you prefer, you can die cut several different options. Lay out the stems and leaves randomly, then position the flowers and follow the steps for needle felting on pages 40 and 41 to attach everything to the surface. Then needle felt fine wisps of various shades of green wool into the stems and leaves to create veins in the leaves and depth in the stems. Embroider French knots randomly around the flowers for further decorative detail (see page 42).

7 Make some small beads for the 3D flower centres by following the steps for making a bead on page 39. Remember that the bigger and thicker the length of wool, the bigger the beads, so you will need to keep the wisps of fleece short and fine for the flower centres in this project.

8 Now fix the 3D flowers, felt bead centres and leaves into place using a hot glue gun.

The two photographs above show the 3D flower and leaf embellishments that sit proud of the felt background.

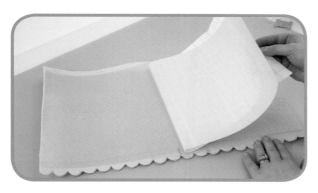

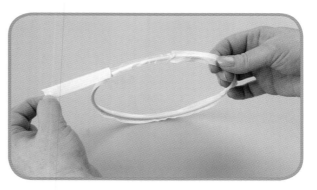

9 NB: for clarity, steps 9–12 are worked on an unembellished shade. Apply the sticky side of the self-adhesive sheet down onto the flat felt, leaving the appropriate amount of space at the top edge for tucking over the top lamp ring.

10 Fix double-sided sticky tape around the edge of the top ring (not the ring that holds the light bulb).

11 Now add sticky tape over the bottom ring. Leaving at least 1cm (½in) above the top ring and the scalloped edge overhanging at the bottom edge, carefully place both rings onto the felt so that they are straight. Gently roll the two rings so that they adhere to the felt and the first short edge of the felt meets the other short edge.

12 Using the glue gun, stick the top edge of the shade over the lamp ring, gradually working your way round the circumference.

13 To finish, glue down the length of the join, which will be at the back of the design.

You can add a contrasting decorative panel (see right) over the seam if you wish. Simply cut another strip of felt, lay it over the seam and match the scallop shape at the bottom. Fix with hot glue or by overstitching either side.

Patchwork Lampshade

This is a variation on the Tigerlily lampshade that offers flexibility and the chance to use up leftover pieces of felt from other projects if you have some.

1 Follow the steps for making flat felt on pages 16–21 or use leftover scraps of felt. The size will depend on your lamp size. I made sixteen squares of 3.5 x 3.5cm ($1^3/_8$ x $1^3/_8$in) to allow for offsetting the top two rows, and six rectangles of 3.5 x 4.5cm ($1^3/_8$ x $1^3/_4$in) to allow for the scalloped edge on the bottom row. Cut the number of squares you require.

2 Create the scalloped edge for the six rectangles that go across the bottom of the design. The sewn length of these will be a little longer than the regular squares to allow for the overlap of the scalloped edge at the bottom. Use the template for the sewing case roof, as this makes three full scallops with a half at either end.

3 Sew the scalloped shapes together so that three full scallops are visible along the edge of each rectangle.

4 You will need to trim off the overhang from the seam on the scalloped shape, once sewn.

5 Now sew a row of squares long enough to go around the circumference of the ring, allowing for offsetting, then sew this strip to the first strip with the scalloped edge. Make another strip of squares for the top row of the lampshade, then sew this row to the other two, offsetting it as before to create the patchwork effect.

Finished size

**21cm high x 51cm circumference
(8¼in high x 20in circumference)**

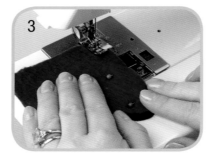

6 Follow steps 9–13 on page 71 to build the lampshade, matching up the edges and trimming off any excess.

7 Make flat felt for the 3D flowers in the colours of your choice, or use leftover felt from previous projects and cut out the number of flower shapes you need, using the template on the foldout sheet. Make the same number of small felt beads following the steps on page 39. Finish by gluing on a flower in the centre of each patch with a felted bead in the centre of each flower.

Tilly Little's Tea Light Bowl

This gorgeous little tea light bowl will give off a warm glow to any room. Use an orange tea light to make it extra cosy. You need to work around a 'resist' or vinyl template to make it.

Finished size

7 x 33cm (3 x 12½in)

What you need

For the main bowl:

- 50–75g of merino in heather
- Vinyl flooring offcut and template
- Bubble wrap
- Hot glue gun

For the flower embellishment:

- Oddments of felt in colours to match the bowl
- Paper template for flowers
- Approximately 12 flat-back pearls
- Battery-operated tea light

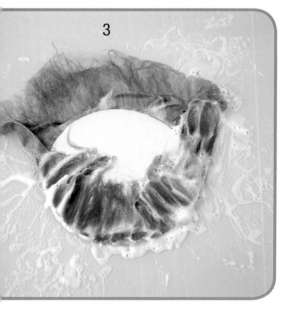

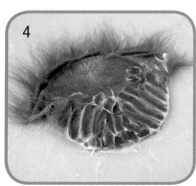

1 Use the Tilly Little circle template included on the foldout sheet and draw the template onto a vinyl floor offcut and cut it out. Vinyl is used for this project because it is thicker than plastic and helps to make the finished 3D shape. Lay the fleece around the edge of the vinyl template about halfway in to the centre, with some overhang at the edges. Make sure that you follow the rim of the vinyl template. The fleece here is neither laid horizontally nor vertically, but in an outward direction around the circumference.

2 Once you have covered the rim, you will need to fill the centre of the vinyl template. Lay the first layer horizontally and the second layer vertically, making sure the gap in the centre is filled in.

3 Felt in the same way as described for working around a resist on pages 24 and 25.

4 Make sure that each time you turn the vinyl template over, you tuck the edges in and repeat the same process for laying the fleece as above. When you come to the last layer, continue to lay the wool horizontally and vertically to close the gap. Then follow the steps for rinsing and rolling (see page 26).

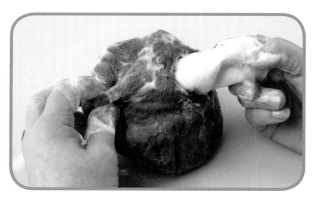

5 The cutting out for the bowl is slightly different to the other projects because it is round. First cut a small snip in the centre and then start to cut out a small circle shape.

6 At this stage, keep it small but big enough to remove the template. Once removed, you can see if you need to cut the hole bigger. NB: be careful not to widen the opening too much at this stage, as it will stretch when felted.

7 Add lots of soapy water and soap and start to felt the rim of the hole. As this widens, you should be able to get your hand in and start working the felt up into its bowl shape. This process will take some time, so be patient.

8 You need to push your fist into the bowl itself and push out the sides. Pull upwards to start creating the shape from the inside and felt the outside. Make sure that the bowl is kept very soapy and wet while felting.

9 When the bowl feels firm and you are happy with the shape, rinse it well in warm or cold water. Put the tap on as full as you can without it spraying everywhere and let the water blast straight into the centre of the bowl and fill it up. Stabilise the bowl by holding the rim, so it does not lose shape while you are rinsing.

10 Then stuff the bowl bit by bit with chunks of bubble wrap, pushing it right in, and compact it so that it pushes the felt into a nice even bowl shape. Leave it to dry overnight.

11 Once dry, you can cut the side vents. Keep them narrow and even. You may want to measure each vent equally if you are not confident of doing it by eye. Start anywhere around the bowl, pushing one of the sharp ends of your scissors to start the slit near the bottom. Then cut upwards, making sure you leave a rim of approximately 1–2cm (½–¾in). Decide how wide you want each vent to be; my advice is to keep these narrow or you might not get the desired effect. Continue to cut in the same way as you did for the first opening, keeping it close to the first cut. Keep cutting the vents evenly around the bowl until you come back to where you started.

12 Felt each vent with plenty of soapy water and soap. Keep pulling the bowl back into shape periodically, as it will want to droop after you have cut the vents. Soap up and down each vent and make sure that each one has very smooth edges. Use your fingers to felt in between the cut areas and get those felted. When fully felted, rinse all the soapy water out and use clean bubble wrap to stuff the bowl and keep its shape while drying.

13 When the tea light bowl is dry, finish by attaching your choice of flower embellishments with a hot glue gun. I chose to die cut mine as they are so tiny. If you prefer, you can do a different combination or larger flowers using the templates in the book. Finish the flowers with flat-back pearl centres and insert a battery-operated tea light. If you have no oddments of felt, then follow the steps on pages 16–21 to make some.

Safety note
This bowl is made from wool and therefore is highly flammable – always use a battery-operated tea light!

Lily Bow Slippers

These beautifully styled slippers are not only gorgeous to look at, but they are also extremely practical and very comfortable.

NB: for clarity the slippers in the steps are worked in a different colour from the finished project.

1 Follow the steps for working around a 3D mould on pages 30–33 to make the adult or baby girl slippers. You can cut them out while they are wet. Carefully begin to cut a slit down the centre top of the slipper.

2 As you cut through, you will see the layers of felt. Make sure that you cut through all the layers and cut about halfway down the front of the slipper.

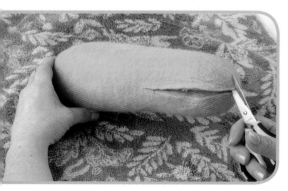

3 Now start cutting a curved line round the side of the slipper.

4 Move your cutting line towards the middle to meet up with the end of the first cutting line.

5 Repeat for the other side so that the last is now exposed.

Finished size

Dependent on the size of shoe lasts; my adult size 5 lasts made a slipper 23 (L) x 9 (W) x 5cm (H) (9½ x 3½ x 2in); for the baby girl slippers, the infant-size lasts made a slipper 10 (L) x 5 (W) x 4cm (H) (4 x 2 x 1½in)

What you need

For the adult slippers:

150–250g of merino per layer (in case you wish to use different colours for each layer) for each slipper in sky, dream and lightning (for the spots)

For the bows:

40–50g of merino in lightning (or approximately 20 x 22cm/ 8 x 8¾in of pre-felt)

For the baby girl slippers:

50–75g of merino for all layers in sky, dream and lightning

For the bows:

20–30g of merino in lightning (or approximately 10 x 11cm/ 4 x 4¼in of pre-felt)

Paper templates

Finishing:

Embroidery thread

Sewing needle

Sew-on slipper soles (optional)

Hot glue gun

You will need a pair of adult-sized polystyrene slipper lasts and infant-sized baby lasts.

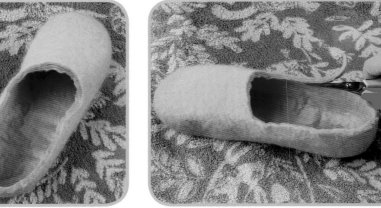

6 Carefully remove the last from the slipper.

7 To achieve the ballet-style shape, you need to cut above the heel line, along the side and follow round to the front and back again on the other side. Do this for both slippers before cutting the final shape and use the first slipper to help guide and match the shape for the other. Once cut, place the lasts back in the slippers while they dry to help keep their shape.

The slippers should look neat from all angles when they are properly trimmed.

Tip

If the slippers are too big, they can be sized down by adding a little soap and water and more rubbing. Gently rinse with warm water until all the soap is out. If the slippers are very big or too wide you can size them further by shocking them with boiling water, then cold and back to boiling. Once cooled, they can be tried for size; if they are still too big, repeat the above. If they are too small to fit the lasts, use bubble wrap to keep their shape while drying.

Adding decorative elements

Once the slippers are dry you can use white merino wool to needle felt some decorative dots. I have chosen to add the embellishment afterwards, as it's easier to keep the patterns intact that way. Follow the needle felting steps on pages 40 and 41. Neatly overstitch the edges of the slippers (see page 43). This also helps to protect the edges from wear and tear, as well as being decorative.

To make the felt for the bows, follow the steps for wet felting on pages 16–21. There are three bow template sizes included with this book: large, medium and small (see foldout sheet). The large and medium sizes are for the adult slippers, and the small size is for the baby girl slippers.

1 Use an erasable marker pen to draw around the templates. Curve your wrist when cutting into the scallops and out of them. This will add more shape and definition to each scallop, as it can be difficult to get your pen all the way into the grooves of the template when using felt. In other words, cut a little further past the indent of each curve. Remove the pen marks with water and leave to dry.

2 To assemble the larger bow, glue one tab of one bow part onto the tab of the other.

3 Then each remaining tab end of each part can be folded over into the centre and glued in place.

4 Repeat this for the medium-sized bow.

5 Glue it to the front of the large one.

6 Use the central band piece to wrap around the middle of the bow to hold and hide the joins. For the small bow, you will only need to use the small bow template, which forms a single bow rather than a double one.

Footman Baby Boy Slippers

These cute little slippers will keep your baby's feet snug
and warm on the coldest days.

1 Make the slippers following the instructions for working around a 3D mould on pages 30–33.
Once you have felted the baby boy slippers, you can cut them from the lasts. Following the
shape of the top of the last, cut a fraction down the back heel and a small slit down the front,
then remove the last. If you struggle to get this out, cut a little further down the front. Trim
the edges of both slippers carefully so that they are even. You should now have a boot shape.
At this stage, you can keep the edge a square shape or round off the corners.

2 Using some oddments of felt from the bows, measure a strip so that it goes from the front on
one side all the way round the back to the other side at the front. Make sure the strip is even
and decide how deep you want it.

3 Straighten the edges and overstitch this decorative collar to the edge of the slipper using
embroidery thread. Finally, sew a button to the centre front of the slipper in between the two
sides of the edging collar. Sew the button on very securely to avoid risk of choking.

Finished size

Dependent on the size of the
slipper lasts; the infant-size
lasts made a slipper 10 (L) x 5
(W) x 5cm (H) (4 x 2 x 2in)

What you need

For the baby boy slippers:

**50–75g of merino in denim for
all layers**

Oddment of felt in lightning

**A pair of infant-sized
polystyrene slipper lasts**

Finishing:

Button of choice

Embroidery thread

Sewing needle

Sew-on slipper soles (optional)

Hot glue gun

Tip

You may want to add a sole to
make the slippers more hard-
wearing. For adults and older
children you can buy suede,
rubber or felt soles that you
hand stitch on. For very young
babies not yet walking, no sole
is required.

Princess & the Pea Shadow Frame

This fairytale-inspired room decor is bound to brighten up your child's bedroom, or even an adult's room – especially if you're young at heart.

Finished size

Frame: 25 x 25cm (10 x 10in)
Inner mount: 12 x 12cm
(5 x 5in)

What you need

Paper templates for bed,
mattress, curtain and
scalloped edge

Hot glue gun

For the curtain:

30g of merino in orchid
(approximately 20 x 22cm/
8 x 8¾in) and 10–20g in pewter
(approximately 10 x 11cm/
4 x 4¼in)

Small amount of pre-felt in
white or natural

For the mattress:

10–20g of merino in dream,
spearmint, magenta,
hyacinth and aubergine
(approximately 10 x 11cm/
4 x 4¼in)

Small amounts of pre-felt in
white/natural, turquoise, lilac
and purple

For the princess:

Small amounts of merino in
green and neutral

Small amounts of merino in
mixed golds and yellows

Finishing:

Embroidery thread

Sewing needle

Shadow frame

Thick card for mattress

Double-sided sticky foam
mount pads

1 Follow the steps for making the flat felt on pages 16–21 and make all the pieces for the curtain, pelmet, curtain tie and all five mattress elements. When finished and dry, press the felt and cut out a curtain shape using the template. Cut out the pelmet shape, using the scalloped template shape, and a thin curtain tie. Also cut out the mattress shapes using the templates.

2 Make white daisies in different sizes using lilac, purple and coral wool for the flower centres. Use the templates, or die cut them if you prefer. Place them in a random pattern on the curtain and needle felt them to the surface. Decorate the separate mattress pieces as you choose, with a combination of daisies, dots, machine embroidery or hand embroidery. Needle felt all the flower centres with dots using leftover wisps of wool.

3 Follow the steps for making a bead on page 39, to make a green bead for the pea and a neutral coloured bead for the princess's head. You will need short, fine lengths of wool for small beads.

4

5

4 Hand or machine stitch the mattresses to a piece of card one at a time using overstitch, cross stitch and any other stitches you like.

5 When this is done, trim back the card so that it can't be seen from the front.

6 Fix the sewn mattress segment to the mounting card that comes with the box frame, just off centre, using foam mount pads, to raise it slightly off the card. Refer to the photograph on page 85 for guidance.

7 Fix the top scalloped curtain pelmet to the top of the curtain by overstitching it. Stitch the curtain tie around the centre of the curtain. Wrap the excess curtain tie around the rear of the curtain and cut it off. Glue it tightly behind the curtain. The stitching is purely decorative.

8 Use the neutral bead as the princess's head and add long wisps of mixed golden colours.

9 Place them over the top of the head and attach them by needle felting in.

10 Wrap one side up and around the head and gently fix it in place by needle felting.

11 Braid the remaining hair and tie the end with embroidery thread.

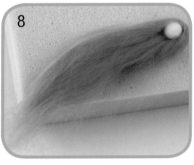

8

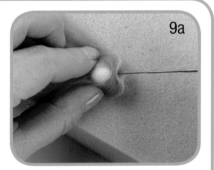

9a

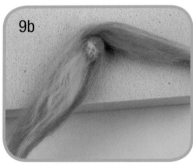

9b

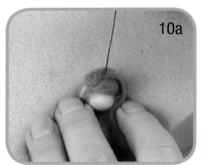

10a

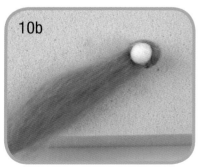

10b

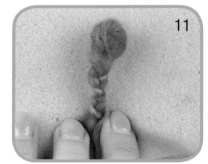

11

12 Use the scallop template for this project to create a blanket for the bed from the pre-felt. Drape and fix this to the bed with very small dabs of hot glue and position as you wish.

13 Fix the princess's head face forward onto the background card with a dab of hot glue. Then position the hair and fix it in the same way, but be careful to use minimal amounts of glue so it doesn't leak or become visible.

14 Fix the curtain by using evenly placed foam mount pads. You will need to layer a few mount pads on top of one another, to get the height of the curtain. Once you have laid the last mount, don't peel off the protective paper until you have checked that it is the right height; you can add more if necessary. When you are happy with the height, remove the backing paper and add some dabs of hot glue to help keep it in place when the frame is standing up.

13

Tilly's Teacups

Hand-felted teacups are a truly unique way to improve your new-found skills and make a decorative project that is sure to get noticed.

Finished size

19 x 20cm (7½ x 8in)

What you need

To make one teacup:

40–50g of merino in pewter, orchid or aubergine

Vinyl flooring offcut and template

Bubble wrap

Hot glue gun

To make one flower:

20g each of merino in the above colours (approximately 20 x 22cm/8 x 8¾in when felted)

10g of merino in mixed green shades (approximately 10 x 11cm/4 x 4¼in when felted)

Paper template for leaves

1 Cut a vinyl teacup template from the vinyl flooring offcut.

2 Follow the steps for working around a resist on pages 24–27.

3 Carefully cut across the top of the teacup from one side to the other.

4 Remove the vinyl template from the felt and trim across the top to make it straight.

5 Start shaping the flat base (5a) and the bowl of the cup (5b) with your hands to give it a basic teacup shape.

6 Cut a heart shape in the front and back of the cup or a freehand wavy edge as shown. If you prefer, you can use the scalloped edge template on the foldout sheet.

7 Now you need to shape the rest of the teacup while you are felting the rim. This is done in a very similar way to shaping the tea light bowl on page 76. Use plenty of soap and soapy water and really sculpt the shape with your hands.

Tip

These instructions are to make one teacup, but a stack looks great, so why not make three in different colours?

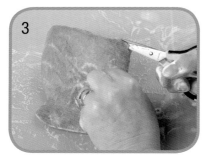

8

10

8 When the teacup feels firm and you are happy with the shape, rinse it well in warm or cold water. Stabilise the edge of the teacup by holding the rim, so it does not lose shape while you are rinsing. Then begin packing it with bubble wrap to hold the shape. Be careful not to pack it too tightly.

9 The teacup should stand up straight on its own; if it doesn't you may have a little too much packing in the foot of the cup. Simply remove some bubble wrap and gently use your thumb to press an indent into the centre of the cup base.

10 To make the handle, follow the steps for making a handle on page 62 for the handbag project, remembering to use a much shorter and finer length of fleece than you did for the bag handle. Measure the dry fleece in a handle shape against the teacup, allowing for shrinkage. Once finished, pin it in place, shape it and leave to dry *in situ*.

Tip

If you want to copy the curved handle shown here, use a slightly longer length of wool than for a basic handle. I recommend you have a practice run first to get an idea of shrinkage. I made all three handles with the same lengths and they have all felted slightly differently.

11 Make the flat felt for the rose by following the steps on pages 16–21. Then create the rose by following the steps for a 'no-sew' rose on pages 35 and 36.

12 Make the flat felt for the leaves by following the steps for variegated felt on page 38 and then continue with the wet felting steps on pages 18–21. To make the leaves, either use the templates to cut out the smaller leaf shapes or die cut them if you prefer.

13 Assemble all the elements by using a hot glue gun. Fix the handle in place first, then the leaves and finally the rose.

11

Wonderland Teapot

The Wonderland teapot is an impressive, decorative project that will complement the teacups beautifully. Make a set for yourself or as a gift for a friend.

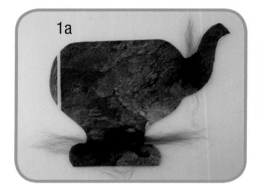

1a

1b

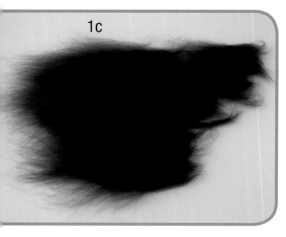

1c

1 Cut the teapot template out from the vinyl flooring. The thickness of the vinyl will help to build the shape. Follow the steps for working around a resist on pages 24–27.

2 When you have felted the teapot, cut across the top, remove the vinyl template and trim the edges straight.

3 Shape the rest of the teapot base while you are felting the rim. Use plenty of soap and soapy water and really sculpt the shape with your hands; get your fist inside the pot and work the felt into shape. You can help sculpt the curves at the foot of the teapot by putting some bubble wrap inside. This will give you something to push against as you further enhance and felt the curves. This process requires time and patience to get the shape right.

4 When the teapot feels firm and you are happy with the shape, rinse it well in warm or cold water. Stabilise the edge by holding the rim, so it does not lose shape while you are rinsing. Then begin packing it with bubble wrap to hold the shape. The teapot should stand up straight on its own. If it doesn't, you may have a little too much packing in the foot of the pot. Simply remove and gently use your thumb to press an indent into the centre of the teapot base.

Finished size

19 x 20cm (7½ x 8in)

What you need

For the teapot and lid:

100g of merino in storm (for the teapot), 10–15g in lightning (for the scalloped circle and dots) and 30–40g in hyacinth (for the lid)

Vinyl flooring offcut and template

Bubble wrap

Toy stuffing

Hot glue gun

For the rose:

20g of merino in hyacinth (approximately 20 x 22cm/ 8 x 8¾in when felted)

Paper templates for leaf and scalloped circle

Finishing:

Embroidery thread

Sewing needle

Approximately 45cm (17¾in) of lilac ribbon

Thick chenille sticks/ floristry wire

5 To make the handle, follow the steps for making a handle on page 62 for the handbag project. Remember to use a much shorter and finer length of fleece than you did for the bag handle. Measure the dry fleece in a handle shape against the teapot, allowing for shrinkage. Once finished, pin the handle in place, shape it and leave to dry *in situ*.

6 To make the lid, use the lid template and follow the steps for working around a resist on pages 24–27. Don't over-felt the lid and rim when the vinyl template is removed as it will be difficult to fix. Cut along one long edge of the lid to remove the vinyl template. Once pot and lid are made, pack them with bubble wrap and leave to dry.

7 When the teapot is dry, needle felt the dots onto it using the needle felting techniques described on pages 40 and 41.

8 Make the flat felt for the rose and scalloped circle using the steps on pages 16–21. Then create the rose by following the steps on pages 35 and 36. Cut out the scalloped circle using the template.

9 Make the flat felt for the leaves following the steps for making variegated felt on page 38 and then continue with the felting steps on pages 18–21. Use the templates to cut out the smaller leaf shapes or die cut them if you prefer.

10 Make the felt bead for the lid following the steps on page 39.

Tip

Making a felt handle is not an exact science. If you want a curved handle like the one I made for this teapot, you will need a slightly longer length of merino than for a basic handle. Have a practice run first to get an idea of shrinkage.

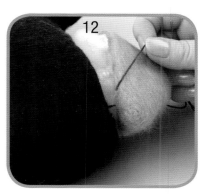

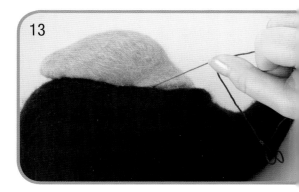

11 NB: for clarity, steps 11–13 are worked on an unembellished teapot. Stuff the lid and the teapot with toy stuffing. Make sure you really compact the stuffing and get it right up into the spout to create the shape.

12 To fix the lid to the teapot, take a needle and embroidery thread and stitch a little at a time using ladder stitch or a similar invisible stitch. Start on one side of the lid, stitching it to the top edge of the teapot.

13 Keep the stitches loose until you get about halfway round and then gently pull. Don't pull too tightly as you don't want the teapot opening to be exposed. Continue with ladder stitch, pulling the thread just enough to close the gap and keep it in place.

14 Decorate the circumference of the lid with some ribbon wrapped around thick chenille sticks or floristry wire. Make a ribbon bow for the front of the rim. Glue in place with a hot glue gun.

15 Add French knots (see page 42) to the edges of the scalloped circle, then fix it to the centre of the pot with hot glue. Glue the leaves on and finish with the rose. Finally glue the felt handle to the back of the teapot and the felt bead to the centre of the lid.

Index